The Ultimate Small-Group Reading How-To Book

Building Comprehension Through Small-Group Instruction

GAIL SAUNDERS-SMITH

Skyhorse Publishing

Library of Congress Cataloging-in-Publication Data is available on file.

Cover design by Rattray Design

Print ISBN: 978-1-63450-722-6
Ebook ISBN: 978-1-63450-723-3

Printed in the United States of America

Contents

Acknowledgments_____

This book is what it is because of the folks who taught me what I know now. I want to recognize the students, teachers, and administrators in the following districts who allowed me to continue my learning even while I shared with them what I thought I knew at the time.

Barbara Eliason and the teachers at her school in Manti, Utah, for the best laughs of my life; and Julie Becker and the teachers of the Granite School District in Salt Lake City, Utah.

Debbie Hagg and the principals, teachers, and children in the Youngstown city schools in Youngstown, Ohio. Especially, Kathy Dorbish, principal at North Elementary, and her staff; Mary Ann Schulay, principal at Sheridan Elementary; Michele Dotson, principal at Martin Luther King Elementary; Maria Pappas, principal at Bunn Elementary, and her staff, especially Mr. Ron Wollcott; Mike Schubert, principal at Taft Elementary, and his staff, especially Mrs. Fahey, Mrs. Hunter, and Mrs. Campana; Bruce Palmer, principal of Bennett Elementary and his staff, especially Laura Sullivan and the others.

Lolita Hall and Debbie Lee, district administrators, and the principals, teachers, and students in the Waterloo community schools, Waterloo, Iowa.

Linda Gehm and Sue Hennis, district language arts curriculum administrators and upper-grade teachers in the East Holmes County schools, Ohio.

Joanna Dodson and Patti Grady, district administrators, and the teachers and students in the Alief Independent School District in Houston, Texas.

My sweet mother, Ruth, and late father, John Saunders, who gave my brother and me our literate starts and the belief we could do anything.

My dear brother Jay Saunders and best friends Jim and Shirley Lewis and John Moran, who have picked up the threads of my life and allowed me to continue to do my work. And my loving, late husband, Chuck Smith, who walked beside me for thirty-two years and enabled me to continue along this path now alone. (ilyfaemfnmw)

Part I
Introduction

It worked! It worked! Small group instruction worked! Who would have thought it would work? Oh, thank goodness, the kids can read! Now what? What *do* we do when the kids *can* read?

Traditionally, reading instruction stopped when children were able to read words. Our job was done. We symbolically told the kids to "go forth and read" by not interacting with them over text any longer. We assumed that because they could read, they were now armed with enough knowledge to keep on reading. We figured they were able to increase their comprehension and deepen their understanding just from reading and reading. And you know what? For a lot of kids, that was true.

But, kids are different today. It's a different world. Kids have other opportunities, other places to focus their eyes and minds. Today, more kids need teachers more often and for longer periods of time. I think most language arts teachers always suspected that we could do more for kids if we continued to work with them.

Besides, we now know so much more about learning styles, literacy development, and brain functions. Or, more accurately, we now have evidence to support what we always suspected. For example, we now know that reading and comprehending are two different phenomena. Reading is an eye and mouth event; comprehending is an eye and mind event. We know that many children can read beautifully, but often do not have a clue what they just read. (I call these kids "false positives.") We know that many children can read, but too many choose not to. These students are aliterate; in other words, they know how to read and write, but choose not to. (Illiterate children do not know how to read and write.) We know that just because kids are in the middle and upper grades, generally grades three through eight, that doesn't mean all of them will pick up a novel and read it, even though they should be able to.

So, we know a lot. And we have known for a long time. This book continues where *The Ultimate Guided Reading How-To Book* ended. The instructional practices of transitional guided reading, reader's workshops, literature circles, reciprocal teaching, book clubs, and various other instructional tactics are addressed here. Ancillary concepts such as text analysis, study skills, comprehension skills, ways to get grades, and others complete the content. The focus of this book is on small group reading instruction strategies that will ensure comprehension for children in the middle and upper grades.

This book offers teacher-practitioners a way to increase their expertise in teaching small groups of children in grades three through eight to read and comprehend what they are reading. It is organized into four parts: "Introduction," "Foundations," "Techniques," and "Putting It All Together." This organizational scheme offers a progression that will lead teachers to greater understanding.

The intent of the first section is to welcome you and put you at ease by validating your experiences. After all, many teachers have been at this game for a while and most have realized more than a modicum of success. We turned out OK, even though we may ask ourselves, what did our teachers know? The intent of the second section is to provide the rationale, or the "why," for doing what is suggested. The intent of the third section is to discuss what to teach, in other words, the specific reading instruction content for these grade levels. And, the intent of the last section is to explain how to do it. Hopefully, this structure will support you at each stage of your understanding. My overall intent is for each section to reinforce what came before and set up what comes next.

"Show, don't tell," is the mantra of many writers. Sometimes, the best way to show is with pictures. To this end, various types of images illustrate each section: photographs, graphics, book spreads, student writing samples, and so on. Photographs include shots of students with teachers engaged in reading, writing, speaking, listening, observing, viewing, representing, and researching events. Often a combination of text and graphics, such as diagrams, figures, and grids, are used to help ensure that the meaning is accessible to every reader. Book spreads include covers, two-page spreads, and expository features (table of contents, glossary, index, and so on). Student writing samples illustrate the nuances of what the student knows and what knowledge the student uses, and can serve as artifacts in assessing literacy development. This book complements and completes the concepts and issues offered in the first book.

■

So, how to begin? Let's start by asking a fundamental question. What is the most pressing question as we consider using small group instruction with older children? The following question is one of the most commonly asked by teachers.

Q: *Should we still use guided reading instruction with kids in grades three through eight?*

A: Actually, what we use is a form of small group instruction. Guided reading is one instructional practice that facilitates continued literacy development. Guided reading is for emergent and early readers—those kids who are learning how to read. The next instructional practice along the continuum is transitional guided reading. Transitional guided reading is for newly fluent readers—those kids who can read and need to improve their comprehension. The next instructional practice is the reader's workshop, a hybrid of the Nanci Atwell model. Reader's workshop is the first instructional practice for truly fluent readers—for those kids who can read and understand a text. This practice and the other practices for truly fluent readers deliberately take children higher in their thinking and deeper in their understanding. Reader's workshops, literature circles (a hybrid of the Harvey Daniels model for use with literature), and reciprocal teaching (a hybrid of the Annemarie Palincsar model for use with nonfiction) are among the practices discussed in detail.

Let's take a look at what happens when reading instruction practices are used effectively in the classroom.

Part II
Foundations

1

Continuum of Development

J ust as humans grow from infants to toddlers to children in the early and then middle stages of childhood, from adolescents to young adults, middle–aged adults, and then seniors, so too does literacy develop. During each stage of growth, specific aspects of literacy develop. Even though humans have the longest infancy of any animal, the fastest growth occurs in very young children. Language acquisition is one of the most rapid developments of human growth.

Continuum of Literacy Development

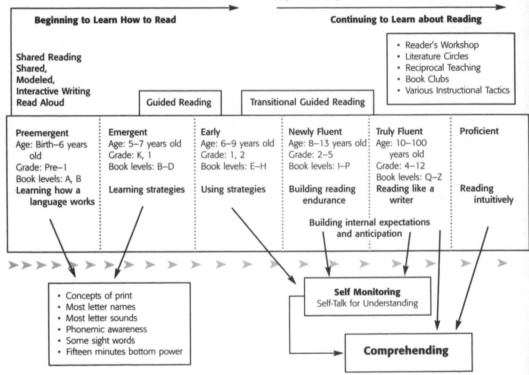

The image above illustrates the stages of literacy development, the types and rate of development, and the instructional practices that facilitate continued development.

Newly fluent, truly fluent, and proficient are the major stages of literacy development for children in grades three through eight. Proficiency is the ultimate goal in literacy. Let's examine the continuum in some detail to determine the stage of each of your students.

Rates of Development

Notice the arrowheads below the stages. These marks represent the nuances of learning. See how small and close together they are on the left of the continuum, how the arrowheads increase in size, and how the space between them increases as they move toward the right. Typically, developing preemergent, emergent, and early readers learn a lot and they learn it fast. These young children learn tiny little bits of information quickly because they are in the prime phase of mental development for language learning. Kindergarten and first grade teachers always remark how fast the children learn to read and how different the children are at the end of the year from how they were when they first came into the classroom. The young brain is wide open to observe nuances of sound, visual association, word meaning, story, punctuation, and all the elements that make up written and spoken literacy. Development slows down and becomes more incremental as individuals pass through each of the stages. In other words, the information becomes more difficult and children take longer to learn it. Teachers of students in grades three and up do not necessarily get to see the changes in student learning that teachers of primary students see.

The arrowheads also symbolize the types of texts students read at different stages of development. The tiny, closely knit marks indicate the length of the texts, including the number of words and pages as well as the degree of complexity and abstraction. The smaller the mark, the easier the book is to read. The space between the marks represents the time needed to read the texts.

Stages of Learning

Preemergent Stage of Development

Generally, the preemergent stage of development begins at birth and continues through age six. However, individuals who are new to a language, no matter how old, are considered preemergent in that language. The older the student, the more difficult it is for the student to learn a new language. The physiology of the brain changes as humans age. Neurons left unused in early childhood, including language neurons, are flushed out by the incredibly efficient brain. "Use it or lose it" was never as true as in the excising of unused brain cells. Some children do not progress beyond the preemergent stage of development. These students become special needs children.

Preemergent learners are learning how a language works, how it sounds and looks, and what it can do. Students at this stage learn how a language works on paper (concepts of print). They learn the code of the language—the names of the symbols (letters) that make up text units (words). They learn the utterances of the language—the sounds of the symbols and combinations of symbols (phonemes). Preemergent students learn to discriminate between the sound units (words) that make up a linguistic stream; they learn the speech boundaries of each word (phonemic awareness). They learn to immediately recognize certain text units (sight words) within contexts (sentences). These five groups of learning are the cornerstones of further literacy development. All subsequent learning is built upon the foundation that is set in early childhood, and it needs to be established in a child's home. Consider that a child has been swimming in a language pool for five years before even coming to school.

There is one more critical aspect of learning that begins at the preemergent stage of development. Because schools are often organized, regimented, scheduled, and managed, children need to be able and willing to comply to their rules. To this end, young children need to develop fifteen minutes of bottom power. Someone once suggested that to calculate a person's attention span in minutes, add four to that person's age. Bottom power is not just a function of attention span, however. Bottom power comes into play when a person is expected to participate in a situation that he or she did not choose to enter. Reading lessons generally last between fifteen and thirty-five minutes, so children need the capacity to endure the lesson. Children build bottom power and learn to endure by participating in many, frequent engagements during the school day. They learn to begin an event, participate in it, finish it, and move on to another at the behest of an authority figure (much like in other areas of the child's life). Try planning a day full of events that change every ten to fifteen minutes. Welcome to any kindergarten. That is why kindergarteners (and often their teachers) take a nap in the afternoon.

The good news is that a person's bottom power generally increases to about an hour as he or she ages. It seems that as the distance between the tailbone and brain stem increases, so does the bottom power. Perhaps the compression of the tailbone that occurs when a person is seated reduces the amount of blood flow to the brain stem, thereby causing the fidgeting in a seat that is so often experienced during long sermons or boring lectures. Good staff developers and teachers provide time for learners to fluff their pillows every hour or so.

➤ *Reading Instruction*

Literacy is a multifaceted phenomenon and requires a multifaceted approach. A "balanced literacy program" is the traditional phrase used to describe this complex approach. Balance implies an equality of measure, but the time constraints of a typical school day, week, and year prevent the equal doling out of minutes per event. The term "program" suggests that the approach consists of an orchestrated sequence of events and materials. Besides, programs come in a box. So, rather than thinking of a balanced literacy program, perhaps it would be more accurate to think of a comprehensive literacy-building curriculum.

Reading and writing practices that provide opportunities for baseline, preemergent learning include shared reading, reading aloud, independent reading, shared writing, modeled writing, interactive writing, and independent writing. These practices, however, are not just for preemergent learners. Notice how the right angle arrow rises from the far left, turns, and points right on the continuum. This indicates that those practices continue through various grades and stages of development. The practices remain the same; their purposes, materials, grouping schemes, and results change.

Shared reading is an especially important practice with preemergent readers. The teaching sequence in shared reading prepares children for the routine of guided reading. Shared reading can be a whole group or small group event. Here the teacher talks with children about what the book is about, a technique called "setting the scene." Together the teacher and children walk through and talk about each of the pictures, a technique called the "picture walk." The teacher reads the text, pointing to each word, sweeping along each sentence; this, of course, is reading the text. Books used for shared reading are read again and again over a number of days with the students participating more and more each time. Specific skills or words or patterns or ideas to discuss are revisited during the return to the text. Afterward the children might act out the story or draw a picture, a technique called "responding to the text." The five steps of the shared reading teaching sequence are the same five steps of the guided reading teaching sequence. Shared reading prepares preemergent readers for guided reading.

Shared, modeled, and interactive writing can be done on any kind of paper. If a copy of the exercise is saved as a record, the value is realized because students can refer back to their writing to read and use as a source for writing words. Journals are generally the first tools teachers think of when talking about independent writing. Writing centers offer similar opportunities. Each of the practices and the related materials designed to build the foundational reading behaviors of preemergent learners continue to be used through later grades in some form or another.

Explicit, direct reading instruction does not take place until all of those preemergent literacy behaviors are observable to the teacher. Small group skill work is the specific form of instructional practice for the young learner. Skill groups are made up of three, four, or five children who read at a similar level. Through the years, small group skill work will become small group reading instruction and will include such practices as guided reading, transitional guided reading, reader's workshops, literature circles, reciprocal teaching, book clubs, and various other instructional tactics. The materials, teaching sequences, and group formations change for each practice. Each instructional practice prepares the student for the next instructional practice along the continuum.

➤ *Books*

Reading materials used in shared reading include big books, charts, and posters. Picture books or short chapter books serve as read-aloud books. A classroom library filled with a range of text types and lengths, as well as books for readers at different stages of development, encourages children to be readers. Preemergent readers generally read and look at books at levels A and B. These simple, eight-page books feature one or two words on a page or a single line of text with clear illustrations that directly match the text. Most beginning readers will feel like more advanced readers by reviewing the pictures. Preemergent readers, like all readers, need to see themselves as readers and so must be able to feel successful as readers. An example of a text appropriate for preemergent readers is seen on the following page.

apple pie

A preemergent text. Excerpted with permission from *Eating Apples*, Pebble Books, © 1998, Capstone Press. *Photo by Michelle Coughlan/Unicorn Stock Photos*

Emergent Stage of Development

As the foundational behaviors become more immediate, the responses more automatic, students move from the preemergent to the emergent stage of development. Children are generally in the emergent stage from ages five to seven or during kindergarten and grade one, perhaps even grade two for some children. Emergent development can happen at any age, as with new-to-a-language students or special needs learners, but it always follows the preemergent stage.

Emergent readers are beginning readers. They are beginning to learn how to read. Children are considered emergent when they have basic control of the six behaviors that are developed during the preemergent years. They now have developed the skills they need to continue their learning. They are armed with tools that will enable them to learn strategies to help them figure out just about any new word.

➤ *Reading Instruction*

The same practices form the literacy-building curriculum for emergent learners as for preemergent learners. The exception is guided reading, which is an instructional practice for children at this stage of development. Guided reading is done in groups of four, five, or six children who read at the same vocabulary, strategy, and skill level. The lessons follow the five-step teaching sequence and last fifteen to thirty minutes. Emergent groups meet with the teacher four or five times each week, working through two or three books per week.

Emergent readers learn reading strategies and begin to use them during guided reading. The single purpose of guided reading is to teach students many strategies that they can use to read without assistance.

The five steps of the guided reading teaching sequence establish the protocol for subsequent forms of reading instruction, like transitional guided reading. Again, each instructional practice sets up the next along the continuum. The purpose of each instructional practice shifts slightly to increase the amount of student responsibility and to change the type of responsibility that the reader must accept.

Strategies

Strategies are mental problem-solving actions. Strategies are conscious decisions a person makes to figure out something. Each situation has several, if not many, specific options, behaviors, or strategies that can be leveraged to resolve a challenge. Life requires such strategies. Every sport is rife with strategies. Athletes have playbooks with option after option after option. They study, practice, and devise more strategies. Their goal is to win the game. Learning to read requires strategies as well. Reading strategies provide students with an array of tactics that enable them to figure out words. There are a series of specific actions emergent readers learn to use as they read.

Reading strategies enable students to use various sources of information to figure out what the words are and what the text as a whole says. These sources of information generally fall into three categories—meaning which refers to the semantics of the word or sentence; structure, which refers to the grammatical aspects of the word or sentence; and visuals which refers to the letters and corresponding sounds that make up the word. Strategies are often used in combination. Some examples of strategies include:

- Reading on—reading along, stopping at an unknown word, skipping the word, reading on to the end of the sentence, coming back, and using the sense of the sentence combined with the letters that make up the unknown word to figure out the unknown word. This strategy is also known as using context clues.

- Using the picture—reading along, stopping at an unknown word, looking at the illustration, looking back at the word, and then using the letters and associated sounds to figure out the unknown word.

Some strategies are terminal strategies. These strategies are actions that lead to no resolution or force others to do the work for the reader. Examples include:

- Skipping the word—the student reads along, skips an unknown word, and continues to read without regard to the hole that was left in the sentence. Some students use this strategy so much that their reading process is like skipping stones on a pond.

- Making it up—this strategy is similar to skipping words but has a twist. The reader reads along, comes to an unknown word, and says any old thing to fill the space. These children spackle the reading with odd words that may or may not even begin with the same letter of the unknown word, without regard for the meaning of the word or the sentence.

- Appealing—reading along, stopping at an unknown word, and looking at the teacher expectantly, or looking at the teacher and asking, "What's this word?"

These are behaviors frequently recognized by teachers of students in grade three through eight. How did the students learn to read this way? Who let this happen? Who taught them last year? Before we start pointing fingers, let us consider that many children in the middle and upper grades have had only whole group experiences to learn how to read. They have not benefited from small group interactions where this type of behavior either is not given a chance to develop or is squashed at its first occurrence.

Skills

Often skills are mistaken for strategies. Or, the terms "skills" and "strategies" are incorrectly used synonymously. Skills are isolated abilities that are useful and meaningful only in combination with other skills. Skills are like screws or nails. Strategies are tools. Strategies are like screwdrivers or hammers. Skills and strategies are most powerful when used together.

Reading skills can be grouped into three types: literacy skills, comprehension skills, and study skills. Frequently skills leak from one category into another depending upon the circumstance. The type of skill is not important. How the skill is being used and with what degree of success is what is important.

- Literacy skills include the abilities needed to read, write, speak, and listen. Because reading and writing are reciprocal language systems, often reading skills are writing skills and vice versa. The same is true for the reciprocal nature of speaking and listening skills. Comprehension skills overlap with the literacy skills pool.

- Examples of reading and writing skills include identifying letters and their corresponding sounds, uppercase letters, punctuation, contractions, past tense verbs, pronouns, syllables, prefixes, suffixes, and so on. Phonics is one of the skills used in reading and writing. Decoding is a strategy. Phonics includes all the sounds given to each letter in all of the letter combinations. What the reader does with those sounds is a strategy. Sounding the word out, or decoding, is perhaps the most common strategy. In the English that we speak in most of the United States, it works approximately 60 percent of the time. Sixty percent is more than half, but figuring out only 60 percent of all words is insufficient for comprehending what is read. Teaching only phonics as an identifying tool actually handicaps a learner.

- Comprehension skills enable students to interact with the text they are reading or writing and allow them to make, maintain, and express understanding on multiple levels. Comprehending readers make connections with what they are reading. Comprehension is a mental action. Therefore, comprehending skills are verbs. A list of some comprehending skills follows.

Types and Layers of Comprehending

Knowledge	Comprehension	Application	Analysis	Synthesis	Evaluation
Count	Clarify	Demonstrate	Analyze errors	Conclude	Argue a position
Describe	Confirm	Design	Categorize	Deduct	Assess
Draw	Connect	Diagram	Classify	Generalize	Contest
Find	Expand	Discuss	Compare	Rationalize	Critique
Identify	Explain	Experiment	Contrast	Summarize	Defend
Illustrate	Extend	Express	Decide	Synthesize	Develop an
Label	Instruct	Formulate	Determine		opinion
List	Interpret	Gather	Eliminate		Establish an
Locate	Plan	alternatives	Examine		opinion
Map	Prove	Generate	alternatives		Evaluate
Match	Restate	Graph	Explore		Qualify
Measure	Recognize	Hypothesize	Extrapolate		Rationalize
Observe	errors	Model	Graph		Reason
Outline	Verify	Question	Organize		
Practice		Quantify	Prioritize		
Recall		Relate	Problem solve		
Recognize		Simulate	Qualify		
patterns		Visualize	Revise		
Record			Sort		
Remember			Support		
Sequence					
Tell					
Trace					

Skills are morsels that give the learner clues about what the message might say. Learners use skills alongside strategies. One is not better or more important than the other. With both tools, the learner is prepared to interact with a message's meaning and comprehend it.

➤ *Books*

Guided reading books are designed to support a reader's existing abilities, provide ample practice in using them, and offer enough new learning opportunities to keep literacy development moving forward. Generally, guided reading books for emergent readers have eight pages of text, with fewer than fifty words, two to four lines of text on a page, and clear illustrations that match the text. The repetition of language patterns, controlled introduction of new vocabulary, ample use of sight words, and use of familiar or high interest concepts form the structures of emergent guided reading books. Emergent readers generally use books at levels B, C, and D. See the following example of a guided reading book for this stage of development.

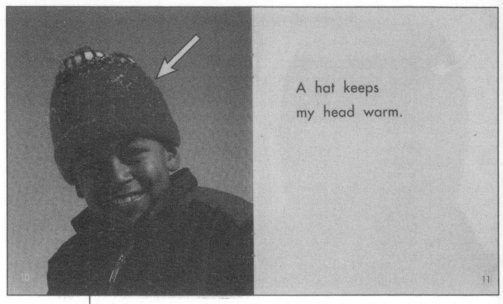

A hat keeps
my head warm.

An emergent text. Excerpted with permission from *Warm Clothes*, Pebble Books, ©
1998, Capstone Press. *Photo by Chromosohm, Inc.*

Early Stage of Development

Once children have learned reading strategies and skills and begin to
use them more and more automatically, they have moved to the third
stage of development. The early stage of development is when emergent
behaviors thicken, strengthen, and become more immediate. Early readers are those who use multiple strategies on the fly, almost without thinking. They are typically six to nine years of age and may be in first through
third grade.

➤ *Reading Instruction*

Early readers continue their reading development through guided reading lessons, still in groups of four to six children who read at the same
level. The lessons follow the same teaching sequence as the sequence used
for emergent readers and may last twenty to thirty minutes. Groups of
early readers might meet with the teacher three or four times each week.

The instructional emphasis for these readers is on being aware of the
strategic decisions they make as they process print. Metacognitive talk
helps students recognize the decisions they make. Metacognitive talk refers
to a group conversation in which the teacher engages readers with ques-

tions and prompts that encourage the readers to verbalize how they did what they did. In other words, metacognitive talk gets students to discuss their own strategy use. Such talk during a lesson helps readers realize what they have done and enables them to articulate their thinking. If they talk about the strategies they used to read a passage and the consequences of those actions, they are more likely to use these strategies again.

Early readers are children who begin to monitor their own reading. Self-monitoring is the threshold, or first step, of comprehension. Essentially, self-monitoring is the conversation a reader has with him- or herself while reading. It is the nearly silent, subconscious chatter learners use to read and make meaning from the words. Most readers are not even aware they do it. This self-monitoring chatter is more than self-talk. It is what keeps readers moving through the print. It is what helps a reader initiate an image and then keep the film moving. More importantly, however, self-monitoring is a security system. Readers who self-monitor realize when they have made a mistake. They realize when something doesn't make sense. They recognize when an error has been made. They know how to the right the wrong and they take the time to do it.

➤ *Books*
Books for early readers are generally levels E, F, G, and H. They have more lines of text on a page, perhaps four to six. The sentences become longer, more complex, and compound. The books are longer, perhaps twelve to twenty-four pages, with more details about character, setting, and action. The vocabulary begins to incorporate more adjectives and more powerful verbs.

Readers at this stage of development begin to develop personal tastes in reading materials. This is not to imply that younger children do not have favorite topics or types of books, but early readers have had more experience being a reader. This know-how begins to shape patterns of enjoyment. Early readers become more critical in their reading. Teachers of early readers have an important job in making sure that readers continue to develop a sense of being a successful reader, develop personal taste in reading materials, and self-monitor as they read.

Newly Fluent Stage of Development
The newly fluent stage of development follows the emergent and early stages. This stage of development lasts the longest, years for some chil-

dren. Typically, children can be newly fluent from age eight to thirteen. Some children move from the early stage to the newly fluent stage as early as second grade. Third grade is the watershed year for newly fluent development for most children. More children become newly fluent in grade four and some not until grade six. Middle schools are full of newly fluent readers and writers. Newly fluent children in grades seven and above are considered struggling readers. Some children reach their potential somewhere along the newly fluent stage and do not become truly fluent.

It is true that each stage of development serves specific purposes in literacy development; however, the newly fluent stage might just be the most worrisome for teachers. While many children, if not most, pass straight through the newly fluent stage of development to become truly fluent, some children encounter several challenges.

Newly Fluent Behaviors

How do you know if a child has moved into the newly fluent stage? Like each stage of development, the newly fluent stage is marked by observable reading behaviors. Newly fluent readers can pretty much read all the words in books appropriate to their age. They have automatic control of reading strategies. Learners in this stage are often described as children who "are good readers," who "read well," who "read fast and accurately," and who "read with expression." In other words, these children are "pretty readers."

Newly fluent readers begin to write with some fluency as well. What they read begins to influence what they write. Their language is more like the written word than the spoken word. Dialogue may begin to appear. A whisper of voice may emerge. Cohesion of ideas begins to appear in the form of paragraphs, whether or not the mechanics of indentions appear. The learner's writing becomes full-bodied with a clear beginning, middle, and end. Imagery, literary language, and stylistic devices begin to give the writing texture. Newly fluent readers begin to write like writers. It is as important now, as ever, for teachers not to be blinded by sloppy penmanship or the errors of convention children may make at this stage of development. As a reader of student writing, teachers must be diligent in reading what the composition says and not be swayed by how it looks. Consider the following writing examples.

One sunny morning a puppy was born in a little coutige in the contrey he was a vary little puppy who was brown and while he trid to grow bat he couldn't trying to growl made him tird so he took a nap zzzzz when he woke up he trid to growl agin but he faild

Name: _____ Date: _____

why can't I growl he said
"you will some day" said his mother
"no I wont" he said
wait and see" said his mother
that tonight he made
sure evrey was a sleep and evrey one was so he trid to growl and he did and he woke up evrey one they wer so prod they gave him a treat! !

This writing sample includes dialogue, a beginning, a middle, an end, and imagery.

I Like Brittany Butt She Has A Boy fhahd and I think She Dot Like me I Like Her so mush I Like her the Frst time I Seeh Her

I Love and I Litz my mom and Dad and famle a God She is my Gril fhahd to me She will Be soh my mom sad I is pepey Love hot to me This is rll Love

To bax my Love for Brittany bas Shattered in The pits of Hell my mom was Right it was pepey Love it All Be sah Whih we wheat She was Talking aBalt Mal. He was Talking aBatt her to I sabe sem thing in His Bak. She Talking A Batt me. We went to ofes that Wahat Hapend.

This writing sample exhibits the voice, literary language, and passion of the writer.

17

Dear mom,
I let another big toot.
and it was funny wene
we got it back Jimmy and
I notest that the stinky
smelly nasty discasting
mor-bid toot had folloed me→

to the room and man
did it stinke bad. I just
a dbat passetout. I knowall
my leters in cursive
Aa Bb Cc DdEe
Gg Hh Ii Jj Kk

This writing sample showcases the voice and imagery of the writer.

See how these newly fluent writers have adopted traits from the authors they have read.

Notice how rich the writing is, how clearly it reads, and how smoothly the text moves like a video or monologue. If these pieces were read aloud and not seen, a listener would not detect the spelling, punctuation, and indenting errors.

Many, if not most, children move straight through the newly fluent stage of literacy development to the next stage of development, the truly fluent stage, and then reach proficiency. Newly fluent readers may be the most vulnerable readers of all. So much can go wrong.

Types of Newly Fluent Readers

Newly fluent readers fall into six categories—aliterate, false positive, social, occasional, functional, and pleasurable. These categories are defined by why students read, what students read, and when students read. Over the years, some students may spend time in each category. Let's see which students you recognize in these descriptions.

Aliterate

Aliterate readers are students who can read but just won't. They don't want to and they insist they are not going to. Illiteracy is defined as not knowing how to read. Aliteracy is defined as knowing how to read but choosing not to. It might be hard to imagine, but some people do not want to read. Go figure! Still, let's consider three reasons why a person could feel like this—comprehension, motivation, and endurance. These reasons may compound, reflect, and induce each other.

Comprehension is the first consideration when talking about reading. Aliterate children do not want to read because reading doesn't do anything for them. In the words of an old song, reading "doesn't move them." Why not? In order for a reader to be moved, grabbed, snagged, engaged, sucked in, or captured—pick your description—by a story, the reader has to comprehend what he or she is reading.

Comprehending readers follow the story, sympathize with the characters, and see, hear, smell, and feel what is happening. Of course, good writing provides the doorway, but the reader must be able to find the door and walk through. How does a reader find the doorway to enter and thus comprehend what is written?

First of all, the text must be on an appropriate level for the reader. The reader must be able to conjure mental images of what the author is painting with words. A reader cannot comprehend what he or she cannot read. Instructional text must be 90 to 97 percent familiar to the reader. The details of familiarity will be discussed later in chapter 4. Being able to understand what is read provides the intrinsic motivation for the reader to want to experience reading again.

Motivation is the second consideration for keeping readers wanting to read. Teachers often ask, "How can I motivate my students to read?" Well, there is no greater motivator than success. Success begets success.

Where does the success come from? Is success intrinsic or extrinsic? Extrinsic programs abound in American schools. Many schools engage students in reading programs that reward students with points. Longer books are worth more points. The points are earned after a student reads a book and takes a test on a computer. The computer currently analyzes only literal data. A computer cannot process understanding beyond obvious questions. So, the questions the students are asked must stay within the literal, low level, on-the-page, knowledge field. A computer cannot process schema-induced responses. In other words, a computer cannot process answers that may vary. These extrinsic motivational programs grant points to children for reading and answering low-level questions. The points accumulate and then the students are able to shop for trinkets in a school store. Success here is measured in the number of points earned and the amount of stuff acquired. Remove the reward and you remove the success; remove the success and you remove the motivation.

Intrinsic motivation, however, exists inside the reader. The intrinsically motivated reader reads because the reading is reward enough. How can reading be a reward in itself? You get no material goods. Except getting to go where the story is, see what the characters see, and do things you would never otherwise get to do. Entering the story gives the reader pleasure. Once more, comprehending what is read breeds success, which breeds motivation.

Readers' lack of endurance is the third challenge teachers encounter in offsetting aliteracy. The reader must have fortitude to stick with the reading. A reader will become exhausted reading a text that is too difficult. A reader may become tired wading through pages and pages of small print. A reader may wear out chasing a story that goes on and on. All too often, kids quit reading because they aren't good at it. They are not good at it because they have been asked to read things that are too hard or too long or irrelevant. The allure of a thick book often becomes the bane of an aspiring reader and the germ of an aliterate one. All readers want a story to reach closure. Readers must be strong enough to stick with the text to the end. Comprehending the text offers continued success, which provides motivation to keep on reading and, in turn, endurance is developed. Children become stronger readers during the newly fluent stage of development.

False Positive

Another easily recognized type of newly fluent reader is the false positive. This reader was alluded to at the beginning of this chapter. These are the "good readers," "expressive readers," and "pretty readers." They read fast and accurately, perhaps even with expression. But they don't have a clue about what they've read. These children blow through punctuation, reading until they run out of air, stopping only to gulp a breath, and then off they go racing with the words until they shout, "I'm done!" As if reading the words themselves would save these readers or provide an honor of some sort. Then, to check to see if they understood what they've read, their teachers ask, "What color was his boat?" And they reply, "What boat?" This response makes a teacher want to cry. False positive readers read like some people eat cookies. They gulp them all down in a hurry, not tasting a one.

The odd thing about their behavior is that they read the text. How can they read it without knowing what they've read? False positive children seem to have a quirky ability to do two things at once. They can move their eyes over print and even coordinate their mouth to say what their eyes see, but their brains are thinking about something totally different. False positive children need to learn to think about what they are reading while they are reading it. They need to learn to include their thinking brains in the reading process. Transitional guided reading helps students do this.

Social Readers

These children read because of the social considerations involved. Though this stereotype is not true of all girls, often girls fall into this group. Social readers' pivotal reason for reading is not to enjoy, comprehend, or learn from what they read. The reason they read is to be *seen* reading or to carry around the current fashionable book being read by all the right people. Social readers are those who read whatever is popular, whether because of a pop culture craze or marketing campaign. Teen magazines, books with pop stars as characters, or biographies of rock and movie stars are often read by social readers. Books with excellent marketing campaigns frequently are the stuff of social readers. The *Harry Potter* books are examples of the types of books social readers enjoy. Books such as *Holes* are favored by social readers as well.

It may appear at first that social readers are superficial consumers of popular texts, reading for all the wrong reasons. Yet, series of books such as *Goosebumps*, the Mary Kate and Ashley Olsen books, and the Cam Jansen titles have their place in the scheme of reading development. The recurring characters and familiar plot structures offer support to newly fluent readers. Students build endurance as they read texts that become increasingly familiar over time. And, the content of such series is intended for general audiences.

Occasional Readers

As a group, these readers are close cousins to aliterate readers. Occasional readers read only when they *have* to. They read when there is nothing else to do. These readers thumb through magazines in waiting rooms. They read as a last resort. They read the directions only when they have tried and failed multiple times to figure out how to do, make, or fix something. Occasional readers read to suit their needs. They read a found note or a purloined diary. They read newspaper articles of personal interest. They may read the funnies, horoscopes, or letters of advice in the newspaper. Occasional readers are intermittent readers. Reading is not a habit for them.

Functional Readers

These readers are similar to occasional readers, but with important differences. Functional readers read only to find out information. Though this generalization is not true of all boys, more boys than girls tend to be functional readers. They tend to be steadfast in their habit, but their range of reading is narrow. These are readers who read exclusively about a certain topic or in a certain genre, rarely, if ever, departing from their narrow field of interest. For example, a functional reader will read anything he can find on NASCAR, being a huge fan of the sport. Likewise, the functional reader may have an impressive collection of books and magazines about something like horses or dogs or the Civil War—whatever the reader's interest may be. The functional reader is more motivated to read than the occasional reader and tends to read more frequently and with greater understanding. The functional reader reads, however infrequently, because of the pleasure finding out certain information gives the reader.

Pleasure Readers

Pleasure readers are the last group of readers to discuss. Pleasure readers read because they like to. They escape into the story and go places and meet people and do things they would otherwise not be able to. These readers generally move through the newly fluent stage of development and become truly fluent and eventually proficient readers. They are motivated by what stories offer them. They easily conjure images from an author's words and enjoy being transported by those words. Pleasure readers feel what the characters feel; they laugh and get scared. They read because it feels good. If only our schools were filled with such readers, what fun teaching would be. But, these readers would read anyway. They would learn to read and keep on reading, regardless of the instruction they received.

So, when it comes to talking about the types of readers, aliterate, false positive, social, occasional, and functional readers are the reasons the world will always need teachers. It falls to the teacher to motivate and supply suggestions to these students.

➤ *Reading Instruction*

Reading comprehension is the focus of instruction during the newly fluent stage of development; and, as pointed out earlier, there's a lot to this process called thinking. Transitional guided reading is the instructional practice for newly fluent readers. It's called "transitional" for two reasons. One, it transitions readers into silent reading, the kind of reading they will be doing for the rest of their lives. And two, the focus of instruction transitions from making the meaning (reading the message) to maintaining the meaning (comprehending the message). This shift in focus and purpose is an important consideration for teachers preparing students to eventually read longer texts like chapter books and novels. The shift is illustrated as follows:

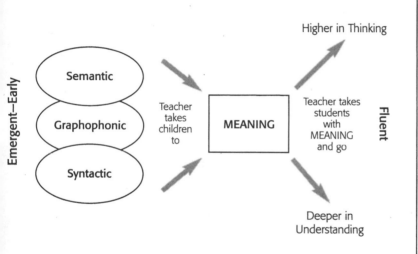

In the past, though as recent as last week in some places, reading instruction would involve students reading a text and then discussing it with the teacher or answering questions about it. The teacher would check comprehension in this way. What the students were being told to do was, "Here, read this. Guess what I'm going to ask you. Go on, read, and try to figure out what I think is important." How fair is this? And what generally happened? The smart kids—those who were good at guessing or who had teacher savvy—would guess what the teacher thought was important and would do well. The other students would bumble along with one part of the brain reading the words and the other part of the brain fretting, "I wonder what she's going to ask. I'm just a kid, how do I know what a grown-up thinks is important? Maybe if I don't look at her, she won't ask me anything." I flash back to Sister Justine's room, sixth grade, and shudder!

And what would the teacher do when the kids didn't respond as expected? Whine! "How could you not know that? You read it, didn't you? Of course you did, I saw you. So, how could you not know that? You are such an eleven year old! Be smarter." To be honest, I stopped checking comprehension when I taught third grade. I couldn't stand the disappointment. Time and again, I did to those poor kids what the nuns did to me. And I felt what the nuns must have felt. But, unlike them, I finally quit checking comprehension.

Yes, I just quit. I realized that I was dealing with children and someone had to be the teacher. That would be me. So, instead of waiting until the children finished reading to see what they comprehended, I started being proactive and gave them a heads up about what to expect. I started telling them what they would find as they would read. I told them what to look out for.

What a difference it made! They did so well. I was so happy; the kids were so happy. They were actually thinking about specific elements as they read. We were able to talk about the text right after we read it. Immediately, we could discuss the material and go higher in their thinking. Over time, this teaching sequence became transitional guided reading. Transitional guided reading does not test a student's guided reading comprehension; it ensures it.

Transitional guided reading groups are made up of four to six children of similar reading skills who meet with the teacher three or four times per week. The teaching sequence of transitional guided reading involves the same five steps of the teaching sequence as guided reading, but with some modifications. These modifications will be discussed in detail in chapter 5.

➤ *Books*

Consider the continuum again and notice that the arrowheads below the newly fluent stage are larger still with even more space between them. Newly fluent children read somewhat longer texts and take more time to

In December, the top of the earth points away from the sun. Less sunshine hits the top half of the earth. It is winter here. More sunshine hits the bottom half of the earth. It is summer there.

CHAPTER 3
THE SECRET COMES OUT

Roxanne, Crystal, and Opal had a lot to talk about while walking home from school that afternoon.

"Boy, Mrs. Charge sure was nice about letting us have the rock back," Opal said.

"Why did Ms. Diamond report us to the principal? It isn't like we did anything wrong," wondered Crystal.

"No, but did you see who Mrs. Charge was talking to when we came into her office? That was Miss Gabby Scribbler, a reporter from the newspaper. She got an earful about our rock. I hope she doesn't write an article about it. That might be a problem," Roxanne worried.

"We still don't have a hypothesis about this rock," Crystal said. "We have no idea what it is and where it came from."

"That's easy. It must be from outer space," Opal stated calmly.

"What?" cried Roxanne and Crystal at the same time. "From outer space?"

"It's not like any rock I've ever seen. It has to be from outer space," Opal explained.

"I don't know about that," said Roxanne. "There are all kinds of rocks and minerals on Earth. Maybe this is one we've never seen before."

"I'm with Roxanne," Crystal agreed. "We should do some research before we decide this rock is not from Earth."

The girls went to the city library and checked out every book they could find about rocks and minerals. Then all three went to Roxanne's apartment. While Opal and Roxanne read the books, Crystal went online on Roxanne's mother's computer and looked for information on rocks.

14

15

Two examples of newly fluent texts.

read them. Transitional guided reading involves texts that are generally twenty-four to forty pages long. Books in levels I through P are considered longer picture books. They are just these kinds of books, longer than books for guided reading, but shorter than novels. The ratio of picture to text shifts from more pictures to more text during the newly fluent years.

The role of the pictures shifts as well. While not officially chapter books, these books include fully developed characters, settings, and plots that are structured with paragraphs to make chapters. A longer picture book needs to be broken into manageable bits, episodes, and chapters. Chapters break when there is a change in action or setting. Books for the beginning of transitional guided reading frequently break into four or five chapters. The details will be discussed in the section on teaching sequence.

Truly Fluent Stage of Development

Truly fluent readers are children who read because they enjoy it; they are the pleasure readers described earlier. These students choose to read in their free time, they read in bed at night, and they read on the bus. They read much more frequently than the occasional or functional readers. They are often seen with a library book and they are often seen reading it. These students are not necessarily the social readers described earlier. Truly fluent readers have developed their own personal tastes in what they read. The word "reluctant" does not describe the truly fluent reader.

More importantly, truly fluent readers understand what they read and talk about it. These readers discuss what they are reading. They try out ideas with one another. They talk about characters in books like they talk about characters on television. These students make multiple personal connections to what they are reading. Truly fluent kids read and think on the fly and are fun to work with. Talking with kids who have read a book and thought about it is a joy. For teachers, it's almost like having our own, private book club—and we get to pick every book.

Truly fluent readers range in age from ten to one hundred and can be found in classrooms as early as grade four. Truly fluent readers must be more than good readers and thinkers, however. They must have more than a modicum of maturity. Maturity in this context has two meanings.

One, maturity means the reader has a respect for the process. The actual reading in the instructional practices for truly fluent readers is done independent of the group. The group only meets to discuss what has been read. Most lessons include a task for the students to complete prior to the discussion. The task generally involves some kind of note taking. Nothing wrecks a discussion faster than a group member showing up unprepared. The unprepared reader causes the discussion to proceed like a cog with a missing tooth. Students need to be mature enough to finish the reading and complete the required tasks.

The second meaning of maturity within this context is life experience. Books for students at this level contain more abstract and obscure concepts. For example, *A Taste of Blackberries* deals with the fairly heady concept of coming to terms with the death of a friend. The experience of having flushed a dead goldfish down the toilet does not prepare a student for the range and depth of emotion in this book. Truly fluent readers need to have experienced a wide variety of circumstances to connect with the wide assortment of issues, emotions, events, characters, and so on that are encountered in these books. This doesn't mean a reader has to have traveled widely or been economically advantaged to be truly fluent. These books can be understood by readers who have observed the complexities of life and lived their own lives, even vicariously through books or media. How long is long enough? In general, a decade is a minimal measure of life experience for the books that fall into this category.

Too often children read books beyond their experience just because they can. Consider the conversation I had with a teacher about how well her six-year-old granddaughter could read. I was interested as well as impressed and asked what the little girl had read that made Grandma say she was such a good (read: gifted) reader.

"*Little Women*," Grandma replied.

"Louisa May Alcott's *Little Women?*" I asked with surprise.

"Oh, yes," said Grandma, glowing with pride, "She reads a chapter to me every night before she goes to bed."

I was stunned and responded incredulously, "Why in the world would you allow your six-year-old granddaughter to read *Little Women?*"

"Because she can," Grandma answered with not a little bit of huff.

"How much of it does she understand?" I asked.

"Oh, she comprehends just fine," Grandma explained.

"How do you know?"

"Well, we talk about it."

"I see," I responded. "So, tell me, you and your six-year-old granddaughter discuss the fact that Jo represents industrial women at the turn of the last century while Meg is the antithesis, being the weak, vaporous femme fatale?"

The conversation ended there when Grandma stared at me for a moment, turned, and just walked away. As I recall, I didn't get invited back to that school.

Why encourage students to read something they can't understand? Some kindergarten teachers are proud to say that they have a student reading a *Harry Potter* book. Why, why, why? The *Harry Potter* books are coming-of-age stories, for heaven's sake. A kindergartener is coming of age six. What does he or she know? Very little! But, parents and some misguided teachers think that little kids reading thick books is good for them. Once again, reading is about the thinking. It's only, and has ever been, about the thinking.

Maturity in truly fluent readers allows them to have expectations about the texts they read. They become intuitive readers. The connections they make with the text provide scaffolding as they travel through the text. They delight when the text spins away from their expectations.

Truly fluent readers are influenced by what they read. They carry away with them impressions of style from authors they have read. Look at what truly fluent writers can produce.

These pieces have voice and tone. The imagery is Spielberg quality. Every word speaks. The writers have a story to show, not tell. Truly fluent writ

An Apology

This is a written apology to all teachers that have had me up to this point, and a thanks for what you have taught me. I was a difficult student, but you managed to live through the experience. This apology is late but comes straight from my heart.

To all my math teachers, I want you to know some of what you said did sink in. I now know that there is a triangle with three equal sides, and a straight line is 180°. I also know that perfect square trinomials factor into a binomial squared, and radical doesn't mean awesome. So even if I forget everything else, I'll remember those four things.

As for history, I didn't learn much of anything. However, I did learn that Mexico City is the capitol of Mexico and the Civil War didn't start to free slaves. The Emancipation Proclamation didn't come until the war was half over.

As for literature, there isn't that much I can say. Except that it did teach me the difference between a simile and a metaphor, and poetry doesn't have to rhyme.

In science I learned many things, but I'll only list a few. I learned how to

tell if a frog is female while dissecting, that most of the things we call bugs are really insects, and paisley (print) looks like a group of amoebas. I also learned a very useful thing, how to make an electromagnet. This will come in very handy if I drop a bunch of iron filings and just happen to have a coil of wire, a battery, and a soft iron core/wire wound.

As for English, I learned almost nothing. I learned a little more about punctuation. I also learned I have a long way to go. Because creative writing is creative. The last thing I managed to pick up is all the forms of the word be, I am sure this will be very helpful in my adult life when doing my children's homework.

As for the special classes, gym, art, shop, music, and health I learned a lot. I learned it is possible to use the band saw without losing my fingers, red and blue make purple, dodgeball rules, and the difference between a whole note and a half note is a little vertical line. As for health I learned that CPR stands for more than "Certain people are Radical," it means a second chance in life. So for all of you I have mentioned, and those of you I didn't, may I ask one more favor? That when you tally up your failures against your successes,

Might I be remembered in the latter category. For although I still dislike math, and punctuation still baffles me, I did make it to ninth grade without a miss.

So to all you inspiring teachers, congratulations and have fun in the years to come. So Good Luck with My Younger Brother!

Truly fluent reader writing sample.

ers are language craftspeople who conjure up scenarios filled with characters that live and feel and interact and change over time. Truly fluent readers write like professional writers.

What do we do after kids have learned how to read and think about what they are reading? Our work is done, right? We got them there—they are in grades four, five, six—now they should just go forth and read. In the past, say thirty or thirty-five years ago, that was the way curriculum was structured. Reading instruction generally stopped after grade three and teachers taught novels to the whole class. Teachers taught novels whether or not everyone could read them. Teachers would assuage any fleeting doubts or guilt they felt about teaching this way with thoughts like, "Oh, the others will get it from the discussion. Those who can read the text will read it and then we'll all talk about it." For students who are not at the novel's level, participating in a discussion about a book they didn't understand is like listening to others talk about what a great time they had at a party. It doesn't get any more vicarious than that. The details of the text become diluted; for example, I heard about it from my best friend's cousin, who heard it from her neighbor's stepdaughter's soccer coach, who heard it from his wife's hair stylist, who heard it from. . . .

Take another look at that continuum. See the two arrows at the very top of the image, facing right? The arrow on the left indicates the beginning of learning how to read. The arrow on the right indicates that students are continuing to learn about reading. This is a different take on the clever "learning to read, reading to learn" quip that was so popular a few years ago.

That little adage dismisses the fact that preemergent, emergent, and early readers are able and more than willing to read (or perhaps look at books) to learn. Just ask any kindergarten or first grade teacher—young children are curious by nature and enjoy looking through and reading nonfiction books to find out information.

Explicit reading instruction no longer stops after grades three or four. As children become stronger readers, as their endurance continues to grow, and as they become more multidimensional in their thinking, so too must the teaching become more challenging, last longer, and include more multidimensional approaches. As students become truly fluent readers, the focus of instruction shifts once more. Reading instruction at this stage of development helps children read like writers.

This figure illustrates how reading instruction for truly fluent readers continues and takes on various dimensions. Instruction at this level is designed to take students higher in their thinking. They are led up Bloom's taxonomy through discussion. They learn to evaluate the decisions characters make and to critique the author's choices. They learn to synthesize and generalize. Truly fluent readers learn to think beyond the literal, beyond what they imagined possible. They become apprentice thinkers, learning from teachers to make connections, infer, deduce, extrapolate, compare beyond the obvious, form opinions and defend them, establish a point, recognize and argue a point of view, and on and on.

Comprehension Subskills
- Inference
- Point of View
- Compare/Contrast
- Main Idea
- Deduction
- Prediction
- Synthesis
- Evaluation
- Others

Higher Thinking

Instructional Options

Teacher and Students Start with Meaning

- Reader's Workshops
- Literature Circles
- Reciprocal Teaching
- Book Clubs
- Various Instructional Tactics

Deeper in Understanding

Content
- Concepts
- Vocabulary
- Skills

Writer's Craft
- Literary Elements
- Literary Structures
- Literary Languages
- Literary Devices

Higher and deeper comprehension.

At the same time, truly fluent readers need to deepen their understanding of concepts, skills, and vocabulary words as well as elements of the writer's craft. Children at this stage of learning need guidance to peel back the layers of meaning and investigate the significant nuances that make up the concepts found in books at this level. Books for truly fluent readers are filled with rich adjectives and adverbs that add dimension and detail to the text. Books at this level are rampant with metaphors, similes, and analogies that deepen the texture of the writing. Children need to be guided to ensure they recognize the place and value of these words. Teachers need to make certain they understand the role words play at this level.

➤ *Reading Instruction*

Each instructional practice along the continuum provides a scaffolding to support the next instructional practice. Instructional practices are frameworks of interaction over texts specifically selected for a group of learners who read at the same level. Guided reading is called guided reading because the teacher guides emergent and early readers in reading and understanding the text. Transitional guided reading is called transitional because aspects of the teaching and learning shift. While still orchestrated by the teacher, transitional guided reading shifts specific responsibilities to the newly fluent readers. The emphasis in this practice is comprehension. The teacher prepares the readers to engage the brain before processing the print. The readers then read the text silently, thinking about what they are reading while they read.

Four instructional practices form the hierarchy of teaching and learning for truly fluent readers—reader's workshops, literature circles, reciprocal teaching, and book clubs. The model of reader's workshop described here is a hybrid of the Nancy Atwell model. The literature circle model used is the Harvey Daniels model. Reciprocal teaching follows the Anne Marie Palincsar model. Grouping, scheduling, and selecting texts for each practice is very similar. What changes are the details of the teaching sequences.

➤ *Books*

Instructional books for truly fluent readers include novels and nonfiction books above level P in the Fountas and Pinnell levels. Truly fluent books deal with sophisticated concepts that encourage thinking and making personal connections. These books are full-bodied and rich. They contain multifaceted characters and detailed settings. The plots twist and turn and are full of literary structures.

At the same time, picture books such as parodies on traditional tales, spoofs, or books written in specific voices like film noir offer what truly fluent readers desire most—an experience that they might not have in their own lives.

Poetry is another excellent source for instructing truly fluent readers. The erudite language and symbolism are fodder from which these readers can create meaning. Many students in the middle grades are poet themselves, expressing their adolescent angst through verse and imagery. Examining the craft of published poets may provide examples of style and language that can add dimension to their doggerels of anguish.

Proficient Stage of Development

The ultimate goal of reading instruction is to help students attain proficiency. As a word, proficiency has many meanings; within this context, it means an addiction to print. Most educators are proficient readers. Think about yourself. Why do you read? Not because you want to; no, proficient readers read because we *feel compelled* to. We cannot be without print in our lives. Like any addict, we think about reading when we are not reading. We prepare for opportunities to read. We prepare for those times when we might have a spare moment or twenty to read. Don't we usually have something to read when entering the bathroom? Should we find ourselves in there without a fix (something to read) we read whatever we find—the shampoo bottle, the bottom of the tissue box, anything. We

Grade Level	Stage of Development	Instructional Practice	Guided Reading Level	Page Count	Line Count	Word Count
K	Preemergent, Emergent	Shared Reading, Guided Reading	A, B	8, 9	1, 2	14–35 +/-
1	Emergent	Guided Reading	B–D	8, 9	2–4	14–35 +/-
1	Early	Guided Reading	D–G	8–12	3–6	35–95 +/-
2	Early	Guided Reading	H–J	12–24	6–12	95–250
2–8	Newly Fluent	Transitional Guided Reading	J–L	24–36	Paragraphs, Long Picture Books	250–700
3–8	Newly Fluent	Transitional Guided Reading	M–P	36–48	Short Chapter Books	800–1,200
4–8	Truly Fluent	Reader's Workshops	Q–S	56–72	Chapter Books	2,000 up
5–8	Truly Fluent	Literature Circles	T–V	80–120	Novels	3,000 up

Summary of approximate leveling features.

slip a little something in our bag or notebook when we attend a meeting or conference, just in case it doesn't go the way we thought. We read bumper stickers on cars and get a cheap thrill when we make out a vanity plate. Cereal boxes should have more print on them.

Proficient readers can go anywhere and do anything without ever leaving their homes. They meet people they would never otherwise have the chance to meet. They will never be alone or lonely. What a wonderful gift teachers give their students by teaching them how to read.

Now that we've explored how reading skills are developed, we'll turn to the dimensions of fluency that ensure comprehension.

2

Fluency

The truly fluent stage of development leads to proficiency. The term "fluency" plays an important role in describing literacy development. "He reads so fluently!" How many times have we heard or even said that? How many times have we wondered what we really mean? Just what is fluency? Fluency is a term that has been bandied about by educators through the ages. It has more meanings than a disco ball has facets.

Often, fluency has referred to the speed with which a person can read individual words. Is faster better? Or, the term has referred to the degree of accuracy with which a person can read individual words or passages. Is correct smart? Or, it has meant a combination of the two—fast and accurate. Funny how these superficial usages of the word "fluency" do not involve comprehending what is read. The superficial definitions of fluency should be a concern for educators. What does it matter how prettily a person reads if he or she does not understand what has been read?

Reading and comprehending are two different processes. Reading is an eye and mouth event. Text enters the eye and words come out the mouth, frequently bypassing the brain. Comprehending, on the other hand, is an eye and mind event. Print enters the eye; words take shape in the brain; they run through a schema and are given life by what a reader holds in his or her schema. Meaningful images form in the mind, which results in the reader understanding the meaning of the text.

Reading instruction has never been solely about teaching children how to read. Nearly every student with average developmental abilities will learn to read, despite shoddy teaching. Reading instruction needs to be about teaching children how to think. This can be a real challenge in an age when too many students are raised in an overstimulating visual environment. Reading instruction has been called "guided reading." It should be called "guided thinking."

Fluency is a complex phenomenon used to describe four aspects of a student's progress—comprehension, accuracy, smoothness, and the ability to read increasingly challenging texts. Understanding and accepting the braided nature of the four dimensions of fluency allow a teacher to integrate the critical aspects of instruction that ensure comprehension into curriculum.

Comprehension

Comprehension has many meanings. It occurs on many cognitive levels as well. Word knowledge is one of the lowest levels of comprehension. A reader might know how to say a word, but not know what it means. For example, a student might be able to read every word in, "The smoke curled in a tall plume from the chimney," but not know what "plume" means. Consider figures of speech, as in the example, "She was always under foot." How successful is a reader who can certainly read the words, but thinks the character was very, very short? Is this comprehending? Or, what about a reader who is not able to read or speak a word but will recognize its meaning by its context; as in the example, "The tiger was ferocious in its attack." The reader may have trouble reading the word "ferocious" but will know what it communicates about the tiger when the reader is told what the word is. Is this comprehending?

Words are the strokes of paint that combine to create a picture in a reader's mind. If a reader can't see the colors, nuances of color, or even parts of the picture, what the reader sees in the picture is less than the painter intended. Forgive one more analogy. Words are the notes that combine to make a symphony. If a reader cannot hear all the tones or pitches, what the reader hears in the music is flat, toneless, and less than the composer intended.

Minimally, a reader must be able to say the words in a text and recognize what they mean in order to comprehend on any level. Comprehension refers to a reader's ability to conjure up an image from the author's words through his or her schema. It requires the reader to maintain an image that may shift as the words of the text and the experiences of the characters indicate. A reader's comprehension remains intact as long as the reader sustains the image. In general, comprehension describes how the reader uses his or her schema to give shape, and so meaning, to the author's words.

Schema

So what is a schema? Every reader has one. Even animals have schema. Every person's schema is different, however. In short, schema is a reader's interpretative mechanism that incorporates every experience the reader has ever had. It is the sieve through which new experiences must pass in order to take shape and have meaning.

Another analogy might help in understanding schema. Imagine that each person is born with a four-legged frame that unfolds from the center of the back. Some have frames made with short legs. Some have frames with long legs. Imagine that each person has a sheet of fabric stapled to the legs of the frame. Some have strong, thick fabric such as sailcloth or denim. Others have thin, delicate sheets of fabric such as gauze or lace, shot through with holes. This sheet of fabric forms a shape something like an umbrella or parachute. Imagine that the sheet of fabric is covered with a layer of adhesive. Some have a thick layer of a strong adhesive like flypaper or rodent glue. Some have thin layers of temporary glue.

Now, imagine that as each person walks through life, every single experience a person encounters slams into that sheet. Depending on the size of the frame, type of fabric, and kind of adhesive, some experiences stick to the adhesive and make the sheet even stickier; some experiences adhere for a short while and then slide off; and some experiences pass right through any holes that might exist. Whatever adheres helps shape, or give meaning to, whatever else adheres. Experiences accumulate throughout a lifetime. Over time these experiences age and crack; like decoupage they become wizened. Perhaps that's why the elderly, with their decades of experience, are considered wise.

Comprehension includes all the connections a reader makes with what the author has written. The reader absorbs the author's words through the eyes and the reader's schema gives the words meaning. Since schema is so intensely personal, readings of a text may vary among readers. The varying personal connections readers make with texts are one reason it is so important for teachers to help students realize that there are no right interpretations of a text. As teachers we need to help children think, understand what thinking feels like, and recognize when it happens. Then, the children will be more likely to keep on thinking.

How do we make this happen, however? How do you get students to think? This task is especially difficult for a generation of students that was for the most part, raised in an environment that included video games, movies, computers, and television. Children in school today have been raised with an enormous amount of visual stimulation. From infancy, too many children have been propped up in front of a television. They have spent hours, formative hours, awash in a visual flood. One can only imagine that whole parts of the brain, those used to conjure—not absorb—images, have grown fallow from disuse. Pictures are conjured from words—words spoken, heard, and read.

Learning to comprehend begins in infancy when a baby is held up in front of a caregiver's face and is goo-gooed at, "Aren't you just the sweetest little doody do? Yes, you are! Look at you—you are so sweet!" That's right, conversations like this instigate a life filled with high thinking and deep understanding. The baby looks into the caregiver's face and responds to the pleasant high sounds, friendly visage, and nice feeling of being held. Who really knows what the child thinks? But, for millions of years, animals and humans have treated children similarly and, by golly, life continues.

How easy, talking. Plain old talk is a jump start for comprehension. Talk is the cheapest activity on the planet. Talk doesn't cost anything but time.

Accuracy

A second aspect of fluency involves accuracy. The superficial meaning of verbal accuracy indicates that a reader can just say the words. Yes, a positive correlation does exist between the number of words a student can read correctly and the student's comprehension level. However, just reading words accurately does not guarantee understanding. Too often, accuracy is determined by the number of words a student can read without error in a minute or other period of time. The only information I can glean from such tests is the number of words a student can read correctly in a minute. How can an educator extrapolate this measure into something beyond the number of words read correctly in a minute?

Sometimes accuracy is determined by having a student read lists of isolated, unrelated words. As if to say, "It doesn't matter how well you can read and understand these words in a context. I need to know that you can *really* read these words without any kind of context, such as a sentence or story. That's the real test of how fluent you are—read these words fast and correct, don't worry about understanding them." R—I—G—H—T, that's good scientific reasoning. My favorite accuracy tests involve nonsense words. Nothing is more frustrating for an educator than watching a child race time hissing and spitting through a list of words that even if they were used in a context would be meaningless.

I could be wrong, but, somehow, to me anyway, a better assessment of a student's accuracy would measure how well a student self-monitors while reading. Like a student who realizes, "That can't be right; this doesn't make sense," and then proceeds to correct the error using a variety of strategies. Something about a student who questions the meaning of a text always makes an educator smile. Maybe it's the concrete evidence that children do think. Children do read for meaning. They expect the text to have a message and they work to understand that meaning.

Smoothness

Notice I refer to the term "smoothness" and not "speed." Reading is not a race; it is a journey through the author's mind. Reading requires that the reader take the time to allow the words of a text to conjure images, take the time to savor the essence of the text. No rushing allowed. Smooth is an antonym for choppy. A student reads in a choppy way when a text is too hard and the reader must hack through the sound units of words. Reading smoothly is not necessarily the same as reading with expression; it is close, but not quite the same. Reading smoothly means reading with rhythms of speech and using punctuation to guide pauses, breaths, and the cadence of word flow. Expression is punchier, more pronounced. Smoothness begets expression.

A correlation does exist between reading with accuracy and reading smoothly. Smoothness results from being able to read without error, without hissing and spitting through words. Reading accurately begets reading smoothly, which begets reading with expression. Accurate and smooth reading aids students as they make meaning, which means that students comprehend what is read.

Reading Increasingly Challenging Texts

Reading increasingly challenging texts is the fourth dimension of fluency. As students become better readers, they make more frequent, immediate, and complex connections. They are able to understand longer and more abstract texts on more levels. Reading increasingly challenging texts means that a reader must read beyond his or her perceived limits; in other words, read outside of his or her interests or comfort level. It is only through the exercising of a muscle that it becomes stronger. In the case of literacy, the muscle is mental—the brain. And, as in exercising any muscle, a person should work a long time within the realm of success before entering the realm of challenge. For classroom purposes, this means teachers must ensure that students succeed in reading and understanding certain texts before moving on to more difficult texts.

Reading difficulty does not just refer to books with harder words or longer books. Teachers can offer students increasing challenges by introducing them to texts by new authors or texts in different genres. Asking students to respond to a text in a different way increases the challenge as well.

Next, we'll explore how creating reading groups with students who read at the same skill level can help create a satisfying experience for young readers and aid the teacher in providing assistance most efficiently. We'll also discuss how a successful classroom routine can be an important tool for engaging students and keeping boredom at bay.

Part III
Techniques

3

Groups, Schedules, and Management

Instructional groups provide students the opportunity to have personalized interactions with their teachers and the learning materials. Intimacy is achieved through the size and type of group. The comparative levels of literacy development among students are used by teachers to determine the ultimate size, type, and number of instructional groups.

Instructional groups of emergent through newly fluent readers generally include four to six members. Groups of truly fluent readers can have more members, but certainly no more than eight. Remember, these are discussion groups—if you increase the participants, you reduce the participation of each individual member.

The type of group is also determined by the stage of literacy development of the group members. The combinations of groups a middle or upper grade teacher might make are endless—a guided reading group (or two) of early readers, a transitional guided reading group (or two) of newly fluent readers, a reader's workshop group, and perhaps a literature circle (or two) of truly fluent readers.

As with every other instructional practice that includes groupings, groups of truly fluent readers require intimacy. As we discussed, organizing groups so they consist of students who read at the same level provides the highest degree of intimacy. The meaning of reading level homogeneity changes slightly for groups of truly fluent readers, however. These students can read really well, think about the text's concept and content, appreciate the writer's craft on an intuitive level, and discuss what they think about what they have read. Because they have achieved fluency, they are homogeneous, right? So, how are instructional groups formed with this kind of student?

Truly fluent readers have developed their own personal tastes in reading. They gravitate toward particular genres and authors. They can identify topics and concepts that interest them. Learners of this age are bound by a collective mentality—there are writers they like and writers they don't. As this is true of the truly fluent reader, it behooves educators to understand their preferences rather than fight them.

A teacher's process of forming groups of truly fluent readers requires a different approach since students at this stage of development are all truly fluent. Teachers form genre groups, author groups, interest groups, and yes, even social groups. Also, I am sure that every teacher reading this book who works in a district has an articulated curriculum to teach. Don't forget that teachers can form groups of truly fluent readers to teach the objectives stated in the curriculum.

The total number of groups is determined by the total number of students within a classroom, whether they are organized in self-contained classrooms or in class periods. Managing four groups is often a sufficient challenge for teachers. Some teachers have reported, however, juggling five or six groups, though I don't know how. Four is plenty for most classrooms.

Scheduling

In general, guided reading and transitional guided reading groups need to meet with the teacher no fewer than three times per week for twenty-five to thirty minutes. Reader's workshops, literature circles, reciprocal teaching groups, and book club groups generally meet with the teacher to discuss what was read twice a week for thirty to thirty-five minutes. Members of truly fluent groups do a great deal of work independent of the group in order to prepare for the group's meeting with the teacher.

In school, as in life, most teachers do not have enough time to do all that needs to be done. The time requirements of curriculum exceed the number of minutes available to teach it. The current length of class periods and even self-contained classroom language arts blocks do not provide enough time for a teacher to teach every group every day. What to do? It's literacy triage, ladies and gentlemen. Struggling students get the first and most attention from teachers. It's not right; it's not fair; but it is what is.

The trick to teaching within these constraints is to devise a schedule in which groups meet with the teacher as often as they need for enough time to complete the work. Of course, this is accomplished more easily in self-contained classrooms than class periods. A teacher in a self-contained classroom can steal a few minutes from Peter's group to finish up a great discussion with Paul's group. This flexibility is not as readily available when the situation involves other teachers who are waiting for your students. While this scheduling system is not ideal, it's often the way schools are structured. As it's often said, "We must live in our reality until we can change our reality."

Management

One of the biggest questions teachers ask is, "What are other students doing while I have a group at the reading table with me?" Traditionally, students completed seat work, worked at centers, or were engaged in a combination of the two activities. Centers and seat work (and homework) are independent practices in the feedback phase of learning, which is a critical step toward assimilation and application. Classroom management requires more than centers and seat work, however. A routine is essential.

As hard as it sometimes is to imagine, most students want to please the teacher. A teacher's situation is like being in a relationship in which one partner says, "Tell me what makes you happy and I'll try to make you happy." The students really want to make teachers happy, so tell them how to make you happy. Establish a routine and teach it like you teach anything else.

Provide students with the opportunity to understand the classroom's routine by explaining what activities are going to happen and not happen. Determine where items belong and have places already established for them. How do you want to handle pencil sharpeners, waste paper, restroom visits, questions, tissues, and all those little items and tasks that make teachers crazy? We need to find ways to eliminate the opportunity for students to strain our energy for teaching.

Do students forget to put their names on their papers? Then put a highlighter pen at the site where papers get turned in. Instruct students to highlight their names before turning in their work to your basket; they won't highlight a blank space.

Do students forget to sharpen their pencils before class? At the beginning of class, ask students to hold up their sharpened pencils. Have a supply of already sharpened pencils on hand, quickly spot-check points, and replace a dull pencil with a sharp one. Keep a second container for the dull pencils. Students have to give you their dull pencil in order to get a sharp one. Some teachers identify the extra pencils with a strip of binder tape folded as a flag.

Are students walking back and forth across the classroom to get to the wastebasket? Or, is the floor covered with bits of paper, pencil shavings, and crumbs of all sorts? Try hanging a cheap plastic fold-over sandwich

bag or a cheap paper lunch bag off the edge of each desk for students
to deposit trash.

Centers

Are centers too basic for middle and upper grade students? Who has
room for lots of centers? And, aren't older students too rowdy to work at
a center? It doesn't seem likely that centers will work uniformly well for
middle and upper grade students; maybe yes, maybe no. So much
depends on what the center is, where it is, and what the students must
do. In its broadest purpose, a center provides a legitimate opportunity for
students to get up and move. A center doesn't necessarily refer to a separate place in a classroom where students go to engage in an activity. A
center can be a box of objects kept on a shelf that the students retrieve
and use at their seats. Alternating seat work tasks with center activities
keeps students engaged and makes the time fly. Let's take a look at some
center options.

Listening Center

What? A listening center for students in the middle and upper grades?
You bet. A listening center provides more advanced students with the
same kind of fluent reading models and read-along opportunities as a
center does for students in the lower grades. Many companies offer chapter books on tape.

Recording Center

A recording center provides an opportunity for students to make their
own tapes. The tape might then be used in the listening center or serve
as an assessment artifact. The tapes can be made in two ways. Students
might collaborate to read one whole book on tape. A sticky note can be
used to mark where the next person should begin. Or, each student
might use his or her own book and tape. The collaborative approach is
a more practical method, involving fewer pieces and parts to manage
because there are fewer books and tapes being used at the station. In
either case, the students must realize that reading a book on tape is a big
responsibility. No goofing off. No revising the original text. Students must
understand that this tape should contain fluid, expressive reading without errors. A carrel of some sort can be used to ensure that the student
has a quiet area in which to read. The teacher should spot-check the tape
to ensure that the students produce a quality reading and abide by the
original text.

Writing Center

A writing center might be used for several writing activities, such as letter writing, card making, poetry writing, news reporting, recipe writing, menu designing, and so on. Materials, exemplars, and directions for each type of writing might be collected in separate boxes. Magazine boxes can be purchased or cereal boxes can be trimmed, covered with contact paper, and recycled to be used as storage pieces. Each student should have a folder to store pieces of writing in progress. A file rack or old-fashioned album or record rack can be used to hold file folders upright. A separate rack will be needed for each class if more than one uses the center.

The letter-writing box might include such items as various types of stationery and envelopes, old letterheads and business envelopes, blank return address labels, postcards, and stickers. Examples of different types of letters should be included such as business letters, invitations, letters of request, letters to the editor, and thank you notes. The card-making box might include a collection of old greeting card fronts, stiff paper for making card backs and homemade cards, tape, decorative stamps, ink for decorating homemade cards, various kinds of colored pens and pencils, envelopes, and other goodies.

The poetry box might include exemplars of different kinds of poetry such as concrete poetry, acrostics, biopoems, cinquains, and so on. Directions or explanations need to be included as well.

The news-reporting box should contain various types of short news articles in such categories as human interest, sports, weather, and current events. The articles should come from various sources, such as newspapers, magazines, newsletters, church bulletins, and children's newspapers. A list of suggested topics to write about will help students get started. Topics might include any kind of school event such as a spelling bee, assembly, sports meet, concert, or play; or reviews of new books, videos, or software; or commentaries on cafeteria fare, detention procedures, dress code, and other policies.

The recipe box might include blank four-by-eight-inch index cards instead of regular size recipe cards since the larger size card provides more room to write. Sample recipe cards and small cookbooks offer examples. A list of suggested meals to write recipes for is always helpful. Suggestions might include scrambled eggs, macaroni and cheese (even from a box), tuna salad or egg salad sandwich, instant pudding, and so on. Other, non-foodstuff suggestions might include a recipe for a perfect picnic, movie, book, class, evening, trip to the mall, and the like. The menu box should include a number of examples in various styles and provide a single sheet that the student can fold over. Materials should include paper of various sizes and colors and different color pens and pencils.

The writing-center-in-a-box approach provides students with the opportunity to experience different types of writing events. Students take the boxes from the center to their seats and do the work there. More students can work at the writing center if all the boxes are available. One or two students might work with a single box. The boxes might all be available at once or you might limit students to one box a day or one box a week. The teacher is the best person to decide how to use the center.

Seat Work

Seat work doesn't have to involve work sheets or workbook pages. No meaningful student learning experiences were ever prompted by filling in the blanks of a work sheet. The last step of the teaching sequence is the student response. There are four types of responses—oral, written, image, and three dimensional. The oral responses are produced at the listening or recording centers mentioned above. Written, image, and three-dimensional responses are the stuff of seat work. See chapter 5 for examples of these responses.

To improve literacy development, nothing beats a healthy amount of reading and writing.

Writing Seat Work

Writing work, in addition to written responses, can also include journals. I don't think that any one topic in staff development programs on writing has gotten as much attention as journal writing. Should teachers prompt or not prompt? How long should students journal? How often should they journal, daily or several times per week? Should I walk around while they journal? What if a student asks me how to spell a word? Do I read each journal entry? Do I correct each entry? Should I grade their journals or not grade them? If so, how do I evaluate them? What if a student writes something that worries me?

Good grief! Some decisions you have to make for yourself; or as a grade level; or grade cluster; or building; or district. You must make a decision.

The decision-making process will be easier if we know why students are journaling. We must have an objective for every activity we have students complete. An objective answers the question, "Why am I having these students do this?" The answer to that question will help you determine the answers to other questions. As you think about your objective, consider these points.

How should teachers use prompts?

Students who only write from a prompt do not exercise the part of the brain that initiates thought. Students easily become dependent on being given a topic to write about. This not to say that teachers should never prompt. Events happen in life that warrant a directed response—local or national celebrations or tragedies, for example. An occasional prompt is a good thing. To help students come up their own ideas, try a process Donald Graves suggests. At the beginning of the year or semester, generate a list of subjects to write about with the students. Write the list on a sheet of chart paper and post it in the room. This should be a living list, with new topics added as they come up. Keeping the topics broad provides greater opportunities for individuals to make personal connections. Consider topics like travel, war, or UFOs.

How often should students journal?

The answer depends partly on the objective. If part of the objective is to keep students busy while the teacher works with a group, no time limit needs to be set. In this case, journal writing is one of several tasks students are responsible for completing. If the objective is to use dedicated writing as an assessment, perhaps a time limit needs to be set. The answer is, it's up to you. You decide.

How often should students write in their journal?

The obvious answer is that writing more often is better than writing less often. The answer is determined by the objective, time available, classroom schedule, and the teacher's educational strategies. Journal writing can be one element within a routine. It might be the first thing students complete as they take their seats. Daily is best, of course; however, students need to journal at least three times a week for the practice to become a part of the classroom routine.

Should the teacher walk around?

You walk around if you want to—but why would you? Older students generally do not need, nor even want, a teacher walking around peeking at their work, giving a them coachlike slap on the back. Younger students need and want the attention more than older students.

How should teachers handle spelling queries?

If a student asks how to spell a word, I remind him or her that this activity is about writing, not spelling. I tell the student that he or she knows enough about the letters and sounds to approximate the word's spelling. I also tell the student to code the word in some way to indicate that it is misspelled. Codes include underlining the word or putting a check mark or the letters *SP* or *CNC* over it. *SP* is the universal indicator of spelling issues; *CNC* stands for "close not correct." When students ask how to spell a word, I tell them to find it in the room, if indeed the word is posted in the room. I do not send students to a dictionary. There are too many words in the dictionary, the print is too small, and there are too many versions of words. By the time students find the unknown word, they've often forgotten what they were writing about. I've helped younger students in a way that may work with middle and upper grade children—when they ask how to spell a word, I ask them what grade they are in or how old they are; then, I tell them to write it like a fourth grader or write it like an eleven year old. They look at me funny but often accept this answer and move on.

How does a teacher deal with the practical aspects of journaling?

When I taught full time, I read five journals each day. This meant I read five days' worth of entries, but I got to see every journal every week. Besides, the students didn't write so much that reading the entries was a hardship. I generally read them at lunch or right after school. I did not carry them home. Each student knew which day was his or her day to have the journal read. Actually, I had an alphabetical list of names and the first five names were read on Monday, the next five on Tuesday, and so on. Each day I reminded that day's journal students to place their journal in a particular place on the counter. I asked them to open up their journal to the entry from five days ago before they put it on the stack. I did not correct the journals. Nor did I make comments. I just made a check mark on the page to indicate that I read it. My objective was to have the students freewrite.

This philosophy may not be right for every teacher. If a student was slacking off and not writing enough or writing well enough, I stapled in a slip of paper with a gentle reminder that I check the journals and they better work harder. I stapled it in because I had a few students who read the notes and tossed them. I wanted the note to remain in the notebook as a reminder to me. So, why didn't I just write the comment on the page? Because I objected to writing on students' work, and sticky notes hadn't been invented yet. Today, I think I might scribble a little comment on a sticky note and place it on a journal page if I felt moved to make a comment. I was cautious about engaging the students in a correspondence. I did not want to become the impetus for their writing. Since I did not correct their journals, I did not calculate a grade per se. Their journals did, however, factor into a participation grade.

If a student wrote something that concerned me, I took action. I spoke to the student and a counselor. In my classroom, students understood that I was going to read what they wrote. Sometimes a journal entry can be a cry for help.

Once the journal entries are written, their usefulness doubles and triples. Journal entries can be repurposed to provide a fertile field for practice with contextualized concepts, skills, and vocabulary words. For example, if the language skill being taught in your classroom is adverbs, ask students to turn to a certain date in their journals and mark the adverbs in that journal entry with a carrot symbol using a blue editing pencil. This exercise will illustrate if students know what adverbs are and how to use them. Likewise, if counting syllables is a language skill being taught in your classroom, students might look back through their journal entries and highlight two-syllable words in green, three-syllable words in yellow, and so on. The same kind of highlighting can be done with parts of speech. The teacher can assign a minimum number of words to be located and marked. Once the words are found, students can list them in headed columns on a sheet of paper. Each word should be accompanied by the date of the entry from which it was copied. Journal entries might be rewritten in different verb tenses or from a different point of view or rewritten as dialogue. The language skill is being applied to the students' own work, which is a much richer and more meaningful application for the student than filling in the blanks in a series of sentences on a work sheet written by a twenty-something editor in a major American city.

Other types of writing seat work include a daily correspondence. Perhaps three times per week my students wrote a letter of some kind at their seats. They wrote letters of request to librarians to purchase particular books or to custodians asking for some task to be accomplished in the room or school. Students wrote letters of request to parents for donations of toilet paper tubes or egg cartons. Then, they wrote thank you letters to these people for taking the time to help out. They wrote get well cards to the ill and infirm. The students wrote invitations to parents, local merchants, and other professionals asking them to visit and speak on career day. These pieces were revised and edited since other eyes would read them.

Nancy Atwell's idea, which entailed putting a check mark in the margin of every line with an error in it, puts the responsibility back on the student to locate the specific error and correct it. A blue editing pencil can be used to make the corrections and it will eliminate the need to recopy. Too often students make additional errors when copying their writing.

Reading Seat Work

Truly fluent readers will read to prepare for their reader's workshop, literature circle, or reciprocal teaching experience. They will also have a written task or responsibility to complete for those meetings. Each guided reading and transitional guided reading group should have a box or small crate of five or six familiar books read in past lessons. Unread books on lower levels might be included in the book boxes as well. Students of all developmental stages need leisure reading, which might include newspapers and magazines as well as independent books of their choice.

Rotating students through a reading activity to a center or a writing event breaks up the classroom time and keeps students engaged in a variety of experiences that help stave off boredom.

Next, we'll explore different aspects of study skills, including how these skills deepen students' understanding of what they read and how they serve students in other important ways.

4

Study Skills

S tudy skills are tactics students use to elicit, attend to, remember, and use salient bits of information. They are routes students use to comprehend readings. A student becomes aware of his or her own study skills in kindergarten while participating in shared reading with big books. Here, preemergent readers learn that reading is an interactive, thinking exercise. The explicit, direct teaching of study skills begins in earnest as early as second grade. At about this time, as students begin to move from early reading into new fluency, students have developed the literacy skills and fine motor control needed to read, discriminate between important and less important information, and write notes. Beginning to teach about study skills as soon as the students become newly fluent allows teachers to make taking notes a natural event in literacy development. When note taking is taught to young children, they grow up with the expectation that reading involves more than looking at words. Reading means thinking about what the words say, working to understand the information the author is offering, and connecting with something outside the self.

Opportunities for learning and using study skills are more frequent and more obvious when using expository texts. Nonfiction texts contain types of information that are apparent and easily recognizable, such as facts and figures. However, study skills can certainly be used with narrative texts as well. Study skills enable readers to attend to aspects of the writer's craft, such as character traits and indicators, literary languages, evidence of tone or voice, and so on.

The probability that comprehension will occur increases when the reader's degree of familiarity with the text is within the instructional range. In other words, a reader will not understand what the reader cannot read. As was stated earlier, an instructional narrative text needs to be 90 to 95 percent familiar and expository text needs to be 92 to 97 percent familiar to the reader. The interaction of literacy skills and study skills and their effects on comprehension are illustrated in the following image.

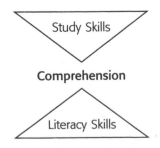

Study skills become a routine, natural part of reading as students take notes year after year. Students expect to take notes as they read. Study skills become life skills. Study skills enable students to do five things:

- Locate information
- Record information
- Retrieve information
- Manipulate information
- Use information

Locate Information

If the information is in the book, isn't it important? A student might think so. Because students are human, and most humans are unable to remember everything, students must learn how to determine what information needs to be remembered. Locating key information is the first study skill. If you cannot find the information, you cannot remember it. Readers need to discriminate between what is important from the rest of the information.

Key words include the most important words in a title, sentence, paragraph, page, or section. They generally deal with who, what, where, when, why, and how. The "who," of course, is the person or item. The "what" indicates what that person or item is or does. Obviously, the "where" is the place and the "when" is the time. "Why" and "how" concern explanations. Key words in response to the first four questions are generally literal details easily found right on the page. False positive children, however, frequently miss these obvious pieces of information because they do not expect any important details to be in the text. While key words indicating information about why and how something happened may be provided on the page, they may also require more thought on the part of the reader. "Why" and "how" information may require the student to use inference or deduction.

Definitions and explanations provide two different kinds of information. Definitions tell what something is; explanations tell why or how something happened. Within the context of study skills, facts and details are two types of similar information. Facts are often numeric, as in sizes, dates, ages, and so on. Details may include adjectives that represent facts such as old, long, green, and so on. Do not try to distinguish facts from details—they provide basically the same information, two sides of the same coin.

Expository features are primary sources for locating information. Sometimes called access or information features, these elements include the table of contents, index, and glossary as well as captions, headings, labels, footnotes, and sidebars. Part of study skills instruction includes teaching students how and when to use each feature. Let's look at the value of each one.

Table of Contents

A table of contents is, in its purest form, an outline of the content of a book. In a nonfiction text, the table of contents indicates the range of information covered and the organizational scheme of the main ideas contained within the book. Each part identified in a nonfiction table of contents is called a section. Like the sections of an orange, an earlier section need not necessarily be read first; the sections can be eaten—or read—in any order. Of course, some nonfiction texts are exceptions, like biographies or books about processes or cycles. And, like eating an orange, a reader does not need to read—or eat—the whole thing; it can be shared. In a narrative text, the table of contents indicates the sequence of episodes that make up the story. Each part identified in a narrative table of contents is called a chapter. Like beads on a string, they must be attended to in order, beginning with the first. A reader does not *have* to read chapters in order; however, this is a much more pleasurable sequence and the text makes much more sense when the chapters are read in order.

Section and chapter titles are rarely longer than five words. Students need to learn to identify the key word in each section or chapter title. The key word in section titles indicates the main idea addressed in that section. The key word in chapter titles usually deals with one of the literary elements—character, setting, or action. Students also need to learn to identify the ending page of each section. The length of the section may indicate the amount of information contained in it. The length of the chapter may indicate which plot point is addressed.

Index

Beginning and ending page numbers are important for understanding a nonfiction text because the next element students should assess when introduced to a book is the index. Generally, only nonfiction books contain an index. The index includes an alphabetical listing of key words and the numbers of the pages on which the words appear. Nouns and verbs generally make up the content vocabulary included in an index. Readers need to learn the meaning of a dash between two numbers, which indicates that the word is used in a consecutive range of pages. I believe that nonfiction books with an index are more valuable than those without. An index offers another avenue of access to the information contained in the book. The index should contain all the important, or key, words in the book. It provides a first site for vocabulary instruction.

By reviewing the index, the reader learns which words appear in which section. Begin by asking each student to select one or two sections from the table of contents. Give each student a strip of adding machine tape. Instruct them to write their section title at the top of the strip. Students may need to add the beginning and ending page numbers as well. Using the index, students skim the list of words to find those that appear in the section they selected. When they find a word, the students write the word and its page number on the adding machine strip. Be sure they know to include only the page numbers that make up their section. As students get better at this task, they can become responsible for listing words in more than one section. Give blank paper folded into horizontal columns to students who explore multiple sections. Be sure the students write the section title over each column and include the page numbers.

Children get a kick out of this task. They view it as a word search of sorts. In actuality, this type of task increases students' attention to detail and introduces them to vocabulary within a main idea context. Several comprehension skills are put into play as students sort the words by section and categorize key words by main idea.

Glossary

After reviewing the index, students proceed to the glossary, if one is provided in the book. As with the inclusion of an index, nonfiction books with a glossary offer additional opportunities for teaching study skills, vocabulary knowledge, and content learning. Two types of words are generally included in a glossary—content vocabulary that is not commonly understood and content vocabulary that has not already been defined or explained in the text. Occasionally, words that have been defined or explained in the text will appear in a glossary. These words often contain the same or similar explanations or definitions as what is given the text. This redundancy is unnecessary and wasteful for students who read the entire book. Be aware, too, that care needs to be taken when teaching students how to use a glossary as frequently the definitions contain language that may be more difficult to read and or understand than the words being defined.

The value of the sorting work the students did using the index can be extended by asking them to cross-reference the words with those in the glossary. Students check off words that are commonly understood, highlight words that appear in the glossary, and search for the remaining words on the page where they first appear—the first page number listed with the word. The students locate the remaining words and find the definitions. These key words are often set off by word, print, or punctuation signals. Word signals are words like "for example," "that is," "in other words," and "as in." Print signals include special font effects like the use of italics, bold face, color ink, and color overlay, which looks like a strip of highlighter tape. Punctuation is also used to set off explanations and definitions. A dash, colon, semicolon, pair of parentheses, or ellipsis may indicate key information. Students learn to skim and scan (skim across, scan down) a page looking for those signals.

Record Information

If we could remember what we need to remember, we wouldn't have to write anything down. But we can't. So we take notes. We teach children to take notes for two reasons. They, like adults, can't remember much of what they've read; so we teach them to determine what is important and then write that information down. And, notes are just that, notes—not whole sentences. Note taking guards against the age-old problem of copying from the book. A possible third reason for teaching children how to take notes is more practical. Note taking is a task they can do at their seats when not taking part in a reading group.

Note taking embodies the ideal that less is more. Notes are information units of five or fewer words—either individual words or phrases. Key words, mentioned earlier, form the heart of notes. Key words from the index, glossary, and text are examples of typical information recorded in notes. These include common and proper nouns and verbs. Other key information includes facts, such as dates, dimensions, and other numbers.

Notes are most often recorded in a list form on a sticky note, index card, or notebook page. Students should write a heading at the top of each sticky note, card, or page identifying the main idea. The page number the information is taken from should be written in one of the lower corners of the sticky note, card, or page with a lower case letter *p* and the number. This information should be written in the margin or next to the heading if written in a notebook. The number of the paragraph should be written in the other lower corner of the sticky note, card, or page with the paragraph symbol "¶" and the number. Again, this information can be written in the margin or next to the heading in a notebook. Including page and paragraph information makes retrieving information much easier. Sticky notes should be affixed in the margin next to the paragraph from which the information was recorded and positioned so they hang off the page creating a tablike effect. Index cards can be left in the book at the pages where the information was taken. Keeping the notes at the point of encounter also makes retrieving the information easier. This process will be covered later in the book.

Here's an example of note taking on notebook paper.

A word about using sticky notes: if your class is the students' first experience handling the notes, keep in mind the human phenomenon known as "novelty." Before you teach students how to record information on a sticky note, give each student one and let them go to town. They need to get goofy with the sticky note to get this response out of their systems. Novelties produce an interesting response. Just know the response is normal and natural, and they're going to do it, so provide time for this and then move on.

Specific information units are generally recorded in a bulleted list. Bulleted lists use a dot, star, heart, or some other symbol to set apart each information unit. Symbols do not imply a hierarchy as do some numbered or alphabetical lists. Only proper nouns should have uppercase letters, and no punctuation is placed at the end of an item, except in the case of dates and abbreviations.

If note taking is a hardship for some students, suggest other methods of recording information. Underlining, bracketing, or circling with wikki sticks (long, flexible, wax-covered cords that adhere to paper and release without leaving a mark) provide a hands-on approach for students to mark information without the labor of writing it down. Highlighter tape is also useful for marking key words or phrases and facts. An edge tab (fancy word for a sticky note ripped into strips) stuck in the margin so it hangs off the page identifies where the wikki stick or highlighter tape is. Marking the information on the page with wikki sticks or highlighter tape is a step that can precede writing information down on sticky notes, cards, or paper for certain students.

Another, but less useful, vehicle for recording information is the blank overhead transparency sheet. A student can place an acetate sheet over a page and shove it into the gutter of a book (the place where the pages are bound together) to anchor it so it doesn't shift. An overhead pen is used to trace or circle the page number and to underline or circle the information units. Opportunities for retrieving and manipulating the information are restricted since the sheet must stay in the book in order to read the note. This method could work in a pinch.

Information from multiple sources can be recorded on forms that provide spaces to note the various sources. However, students are required to think more when they are given a blank paper and told to organize it rather than when they are given a work sheet with organized columns. They need direct instruction and plenty of guided practice with samples to devise their own recording forms.

Retrieve Information

Does this process refer to going back and finding the information in the original sources? Well, sort of. In the context of note taking and study skills, the term "retrieve" has two meanings. First, the term refers to the decision to leave notes written on sticky notes hanging in the book at the point at which they were found. Why are they left there? That answer brings us to the second meaning. Sticky notes are left in the book so that the student can go back and verify, clarify, and expand the notes. They are removed afterward.

Verifying data is a life skill in research. Since so many young people are in a hurry to complete tasks, the likelihood of them making mistakes while copying increases exponentially with the number of notes taken. Double-checking the details—facts, figures, names, places, sequences, and so on—needs to become routine. I know students hate to go back and do anything twice. That's why verifying has to become a routine part of note taking. Routines make things seem normal. We brush our teeth every day, not just on Monday.

Clarifying data is harder to convince students to do. Clarifying means to go back to the source and look for sections of text that will explain a term or idea. In other words, students return to the original text to add specific details that better explain the information they recorded in their notes. Teachers need to be careful when teaching this strategy: sometimes students go back to clarify and end up copying right off the page.

Expanding data is a procedure that is an adjustment on the process of clarifying. Expanding data means going back to the original text and seeing if any important details were missed. In other words, students return to the text to include additional facts to complete the range of information recorded. It also means going to supplemental resources to find out more about an idea or term. Again, students dislike going back to an original source to do more work. When the sequence of purpose becomes routine, their dislike probably won't go away, but it might diminish.

Manipulate Information

Those two words may have a tarnished meaning, especially in the context of business or certain research projects. But, when manipulation is used within the framework of study skills, to manipulate means to move. Sticky notes can't stay in books forever. At some point, the notes have to be removed and the book returned so others can use it. Manipulating information means removing the sticky notes or note cards from the original source and placing them elsewhere. For example, sticky notes can be placed on pages in a notebook or on individual pages or half sheets. Note cards can be gathered into a box or envelope or banded together. Moving information out of the original text eliminates the possibility of student plagiarism. It also makes clear the purpose of retrieving the notes for verification, clarification, and expansion. Once the original text is no longer at hand, the student must rely upon the notes he or she took. The students sink or swim based on the quality of their notes.

Once the information has been literally gathered together, it needs to be sorted and organized, which brings us to the second meaning for manipulating information. Students don't just move the sticky notes and note cards elsewhere, they move them around. Sticky notes and note cards provide the greatest flexibility for arranging information. The information might be categorized on an outline, web diagram, schematic grid, or storyboard. Each of these graphic organizers serves as part of the scaffolding students can use to apply information. This is why it is so important that students take detailed, useful notes.

Use Information

The purpose of teaching students to take notes is to enable them to own the information so they can do something with it—use it. How? Well, to express their understanding, for one thing. It is not sufficient to ask students what they know, have learned, or understand to assess familiarity with a subject. Knowledge is ambient; it floats around. It comes and goes. As such, it cannot be measured this way. Besides, most people in the adult world do not really care about what you know. What matters is what you do with what you know. Use it, show what you know, and *do* something. Another application for the advice, "Show, don't tell."

The four types of responses—oral, written, image, and three dimensional—discussed in chapter 5 encompass what we are talking about here. The specific type of response engages the learner in a cognitive interaction, causing him or her to connect what has just been learned with everything else that he or she knows. The combined and recombined understanding is then expressed by way of an artifact, which can be measured. The artifacts that result from responses offer a glimpse into not only what a student knows or has learned while reading and taking notes, but how he or she thinks, processes information, makes decisions, plans, and executes. The information in a response provides teachers with a multifactored assessment of student learning.

Next, we'll look at transitional guided reading and the steps a teacher can follow to lead newly fluent readers into, through, and out of a text.

5

Transitional Guided Reading

Transitional guided reading is the second instructional practice in the continuum of literacy development. It is intended for newly fluent readers. This practice is called transitional for two reasons. One, it transitions readers into silent reading. And, it transitions the focus of instruction to comprehending what is read. Study skills are a prominent factor during transitional guided reading. Transitional guided reading is the interim practice in which students build endurance and learn to think about what they are reading before they engage with a novel.

Books

Books for transitional guided reading are longer picture books. Often these books have been overlooked as they are wrongly considered "baby books." This assumption is unfortunate because many clever, well-written books in many genres and on any number of topics are disregarded or scorned because of it. Many witty parodies have been published in longer picture book form. It is the newly fluent reader who has the maturity to appreciate the various points of view and twists that these books offer.

The Foutnas and Pinnell guided reading levels for transitional guided reading books include levels I through P. Books at the lower end of that range are generally not chapter books and those at the higher end are certainly not novels. Transitional guided reading books are, however, fully developed stories with episodic plot points, rich character development and interplay, and detailed settings.

Books for newly fluent readers run from twelve to forty pages long. Shorter books, sixteen to twenty-four pages or so, generally break into three or four chapters since the text is too long to read in one lesson. Longer picture books generally break into four to six chapters.

The ratio of illustration to print is about equal. The print is not too small and plenty of white space separates lines of type. The illustrations may contain extraneous detail and offer opportunities for the students to predict and infer. Foreshadowing sometimes appears in the illustrations as well. Illustrations may be somewhat stylized as they serve more as an accessory to the text rather than as a support to the reader.

Chapters generally break when there is a change in setting or action. Often the beginning of a new chapter is made obvious by the text itself as in, "The next morning. . ." or, "Later that week. . ." The end of a chapter may be made obvious by the writing as well. The action may come to a logical close with a sentence like, "They walked home talking about what it might be." The teacher determines where the chapter breaks occur prior to teaching the first lesson and instructs the students to mark off the chapters in their copies during the book introduction.

A two-inch square sticky note is attached to the left margin of the first page of each chapter. (Chapters generally begin on the left-hand page.) They may need guided practice to position the sticky part on the page and let the rest hang off the page like a tab. Subsequent sticky notes are set below the previous note so the sticky notes are staggered along the outside edge of the book.

Teaching Sequence

The lesson routine in transitional guided reading mirrors that of guided reading with a few modifications. Both sequences involve steps that move students into, through, and out of a text. Those steps include:

- Setting the scene
- Introducing the book
- Taking a picture walk
- Reading the text
- Returning to the text
- Responding

The teacher's role in transitional guided reading, as in all instructional practices, is to ready the readers for the reading. Then the teacher guides their thinking during the reading. The teacher directs the readers as they revisit the text to investigate the nuances of meaning, a process that ensures their understanding. And finally the teacher provides opportunities for the readers to respond to the text by interacting with the concept, skills, and vocabulary words and by expressing their understanding in a variety of ways. These steps are the same for fiction as well as nonfiction with a few modifications.

Setting the Scene

Transitional guided reading transitions the focus of instruction to student comprehension of what was read. Comprehending occurs more quickly and deeply and lasts longer if the brain is actively engaged right from the start. It is the teacher's responsibility to mine the students' schema and pull forward the experiences and understandings they have that can be used to help them make and maintain meaning from the author's words. The first step of the teaching sequence does just that. The teacher tells the readers what the story is about.

Recall that fiction books do not just provide an account of a character or place or event. Every book is about some idea. Narrative texts have a concept or theme. In setting the scene, the teacher tells the students what the book is about, what the concept or the main idea is, and what they will learn about from reading this book. The teacher does not show the cover and ask the students, "What do you think this book is going to be about?" They don't have a clue beyond the title and cover illustration. Why do we make students guess in the name of predicting? When you and I choose a book to read for pleasure, we don't look at the title and cover and then predict, "I bet this book is about a woman who. . . ."

As proficient, adult consumers of quality trashy novels, most readers generally chose books we already know something about. We're familiar with the author, the book was recommended by someone we trust, we've read a review, or a least we have read the back cover of the book. This knowledge provides a platform of expectations that guides our thinking about the book. We begin the book with an appropriate mind-set, which enables us to interact with the concept throughout the text.

Students especially need to have a platform of expectations. It is the teacher who must talk to the students about the concept or main idea prior to reading. In this way, the students have a route carved into their thinking before they begin reading. Expectations of the author are summoned and used to shape the student thinking. However, it is important not to give too much information to the students. With a gentle hand, the teacher needs to entice, woo, and court the readers. Motivate them by assuring them this book was selected just for them because of what they know. An example of a dialogue between a group of newly fluent readers and their teacher might go like this:

Teacher: This is a book about changing your feelings about someone. You know about that. What does that mean, to change your feelings about someone?

Sam: You might not like someone at first and then after a while you find out that you really do like them.

Teacher: Like how?

Dominic: There's this kid in my building, he's kind of fat and at first I didn't like him. No one really liked him 'cause he just sat around and didn't do anything. Then, one day, us guys were outside playing b-ball and the ball flew over to where he was sitting and he threw it back to us. He always got the ball when it went out. He started doing it every time we were out to play. We found out he's a nice kid. Now everybody likes him. We call him Chaser 'cause that's what he does; he chases the ball for us.

By telling the students what the book is about, the teacher enables them to call up relevant events and characters that they can use as exemplars as they read the text. The students are now able to use their schema to make connections with what the author offers. The expectations called forth from their experiences serve as a template that helps them form meaningful interpretations about the author's intent. Setting the scene is a powerful step in the teaching sequence. Sadly, it is often omitted from the routine because teachers lack time or understanding about the purpose of this step.

By their very nature, nonfiction texts offer greater opportunities for the use of some kind of graphic organizer during setting the scene. A web, list, time line, schematic grid, T-chart, or TKWL chart are commonly used to gather and organize information the students already own.

Introducing the Book

The next step in the transitional guided reading teaching sequence is to introduce readers to the details of the book. Details include title, genre and motifs, author, blurb, table of contents (if there is one), and any front matter. The first three details can be addressed in any order, though title and author make sense as the first two details discussed. The cover illustration is examined and discussed. The teacher names any characters pictured on the cover. The teacher always uses proper nouns when discussing the characters. Now that the students know what the book is about, they are in a better position to predict what might happen in the story. Here the teacher may ask, "What does that title make you think?" "Tell me what comes to mind when you hear that title?" or "Explain what you think that title means."

It is important for students to think of the author as a human being. That may sound odd, but students need to realize that a real person made conscious decisions about what the book would be about and what it would accomplish. It is the teacher's responsibility to humanize the author. This is not a problem if the teacher is familiar with the author. Books sometimes include a biographical note about the author or an introduction from the author, which may include pertinent information and offer some background on who this person is. A full biography isn't always needed. A simple mention of skill or craft can be enough. Any kind of personal comment about the author will make the writer seem like a real person. As the teacher, you have already read the book, so you can deduce something about the writer. Anything innocuous will do; consider this example, "This author is the best at using character traits. The descriptions are so complete. Wait until you read about the main character." Make sure that what you say about the author is at least true for the story.

The next topic covered is genre. The teacher defines the story's genre and discusses the motifs of that genre. A student's knowledge of genre provides scaffolding for them to develop expectations of another sort. Genre dialogue might go something like:

Teacher: This book is historical fiction. You know what that means. What are some of the motifs of historical fiction?

Jamarkus: Well, it happened in the olden days.

Britney: And the author made it up.

Teacher: Could it have really happened?

Tabitha: It could. I think. If the author said it was based on true events, it could have really happened. But it was probably just made up but really like it was back then.

Teacher: So, what will we expect to find as we read this? What kinds of characters, settings, and actions?

Discussion about the genres and motifs establishes another platform for students to develop expectations about the story. These strands of discussion begin to weave a fabric upon which the tapestry of the story will be embroidered. It is important to remember, however, that the discussion needs to be brief. Frequently, less is more when setting the scene and introducing the book. Teachers need to leave some story elements for the students to uncover, discover, and realize. Remember this is transitional *guided* reading, not transitional shove-it-down-their-throat reading.

So often the back cover of the book is overlooked. Yet, adult readers often turn to the back cover first. Useful information can be found there. Oftentimes, a book at this level might include a blurb on the back cover. A blurb is a minisummary of what the book is about. It is a paragraph or two that gives the reader a peek into the book's character and action. It's a preview; a glimpse to whet a reader's appetite. The teacher might read the blurb or ask a student or the whole group to read it aloud. The teacher might choose to read any reviews that appear on the back cover as well. The content and structure of the blurbs provided by the publisher may vary from the blurbs students would write about the book if they were asked for their opinions.

If the book is already broken into chapters and a table of contents is provided, this material provides the next discussion topic for introducing the book. The teacher leads the students in the reading of each title, pointing out that chapter titles are rarely more than five words long. The group identifies the key word in each chapter title. Generally, chapter titles reflect one of the literary elements of character, setting, or action. The teacher and students may make this determination as well. The length of each chapter is discussed, as are the reasons for the lengths. Some books have a chapter for each plot point. Plot points are discussed on page 129.

If the book is not already broken into chapters, the teacher needs to do this prior to the lesson. The teacher leads the children in marking off each chapter. Sticky notes work well to do this. Each student is given a sticky note for each chapter in the book; four chapters, four sticky notes. Books generally begin on page two, so the teacher shows the students how to place the first sticky note at the top of page two. This application requires direct teaching and guided practice from the teacher. Students position the sticky notes in the margin of the page, careful not to cover up words or illustrations, so that the notes stick out from the pages like tabs, as shown in the example below.

Using sticky notes as chapter markers.

Taking a Picture Walk

The next step of the teaching sequence is the picture walk. Transitional guided reading uses longer picture books, so introducing a picture walk into the teaching sequence is only natural. The teacher and students walk through and talk about only the pictures in the chapter to be read that day, not the whole book. The picture walk in transitional guided reading serves a different purpose than it does in guided reading. In guided reading for emergent and early readers, the picture walk alerts readers to details in the illustrations that may help them puzzle out words. In transitional guided reading, however, the picture walk explores the literary elements of character, setting, and action.

The teacher begins the discussion of each illustration by asking, "What do you see?" The teacher directs the students to pay attention to evidence of character traits and dimensions of setting and action. For example, the teacher might say something like, "What do you notice about the sky? What does that make you think?" Or, "Look at the expression on Bailey's face. How do you interpret that look?" Or, "Why do you think Catherine is looking away?" Everything the teacher asks should take children's thinking higher and their understandings deeper. It is important to remember, however, that the picture walk is brief; here the reader learns to interpret the illustrator's rendering of the author's words. Here, too, the teacher may entice the readers with comments like, "Wait 'til you read how the author describes this guy! He is so good at character traits. You'll love it." This kind of talk lures the readers and builds expectations that take the form of anticipation. Readers enter the text with a heightened awareness. They are ready to read it!

Reading the Text and Returning to the Text

In guided reading, reading the text and returning to the text are the third and fourth steps of the lesson design. In guided reading, the whole book is read straight through. Then, the teacher and students return to the text to use metacognition strategies and analyze content. As the fourth step, returning to the text is the step in which the explicit, direct teaching of skills and vocabulary words occurs. In transitional guided reading, however, the steps of reading and returning occur in tandem.

Transitional guided reading prepares students to read silently and transitions the focus of the teacher's instruction to helping students comprehend what is read. Newly fluent readers learn how to think about what they are reading while they read during transitional guided reading lessons. The teacher's role is to ensure comprehension rather than to check comprehension. To this end, the reading is done sentence by sentence, paragraph by paragraph, eventually moving to page by page.

Before each paragraph is read, the teacher tells the students what the paragraph is about. In other words, the teacher tells the students what they will find out as they read. For example, "In this next paragraph, you are going to find out why Jessie decided not to help her sister. Read this paragraph and be on the look out for why Jessie did not offer to help. Put up a thumb when you have finished reading the paragraph and are ready to talk." I usually ask students to sweep their fingers along the text as they read. I tell them this helps me know where their eyes are. They generally comply. The thumbs-up is a silent, low-motion signal that eliminates hand or arm waving, exaggerated sighs, and other overt indications that declare, "I'm done!"

By telling the students what they will find out in the next paragraph, teachers encourage students to keep their brains actively engaged. A mental antenna of sorts is turned on in the readers' brains. This antenna acts as a receiver, searching for and expecting to collect information about why Jessie didn't help her sister. As the readers' eyes move across the text, the antenna hums with expectation. The reader is consciously involved, with eyes and mind moving together; the reader is actively thinking while reading. When the student's eyes cross the words that explain why Jessie didn't help, then (slam!) the student forms a memory about the reading.

While the students read, the teacher watches them. The teacher needs to be looking at the children's faces to see what they are doing. The teacher needs to watch for children who peek over at a group member to see where that person is in the reading. Or, the teacher needs to notice when a child slows down or stumbles over a word. The occasions of stumbling are more obvious if the students sweep their fingers along the text. The teacher needs to be ready to give a nod or smile of encouragement if a student glances up. Certainly, the teacher needs to be ready to slip in and assist an individual if necessary.

The return to the text or the debriefing occurs when all the children have indicated they are finished reading. The teacher leads the discussion, "So, why did Jessie decide not to help her sister?" Here the children respond by talking about what they found out in the paragraph. This discussion is not just a dialogue of the literal aspects of the text. The first response may be literal, but the teacher leads the discussion off the page into the realms of inference, deduction, prediction, cause, effect, and so on. The teacher might then ask the students, "So, what does that make you think about Jessica?" The teacher drives the students back into what they already know about the characters or actions with questions like, "How does this fit with what she did with the neighbor lady in the beginning of the story?" The teacher constantly helps students make connections with their own lives, other books, and the real world by prompting with statements like, "Think of a time when you were in a similar situation. What did you decide to do?"

If students are unable to make connections, the teacher guides them, as in, "This reminds me of the kid in *Night Queen's Blue Velvet Dress*. Think about how he felt about helping." Sometimes students need a hand making the connections. They may make these connections if the teacher introduces a familiar story or personal vignette. Remember, this is transitional *guided* reading, students still need to be guided. Newly fluent students are learning how to think. They are learning what thinking feels like and they are learning to recognize when it happens and what it can do for them.

Some teachers may wonder if the "set 'em up, set 'em to it" debriefing routine slows down the reading. Of course it does! That's the point. By telling the students what they will find, watching them read silently, and then talking about the reading, teachers allow students to feel what thinking while reading is like. Remember, newly fluent readers are the most vulnerable to literacy maladies, including the "read really fast, blow through punctuation, and get done first" syndrome.

So, do students ever read out loud during transitional guided reading? I have to ask, why would they? Some teachers might ask, "Well, how will I know what strategies they are using?" To this I reply, "If you have any doubts about how well the students are reading or which strategies they are using, either they are not newly fluent or you don't trust them or you don't trust yourself." Teachers should not use transitional guided reading strategies with students who we think may not be newly fluent. If you think they may not be, they probably aren't.

Another concern about students being allowed to read aloud is, "But they *like* to read out loud." To this I reply, So what? Teaching is not about doing what students like; it is about providing them with what they need, and learning to do what's needed rather than what's liked is a lesson best learned young. This is reading instruction. We use transitional guided reading strategies because newly fluent readers need to learn to read silently and think about what they are reading while they are reading. They have twenty-three and a half hours of each day to read aloud to someone.

Of course there will be times when students read aloud. Often the teacher will ask the student to "read the part that tells you . . ." or "read how the author describes . . ." The teacher may even ask the whole group to read aloud a short paragraph or section to pick up the pace of the discussion. The important thing to remember is the reason you are asking students to do what you are asking them to do.

This routine of reading the text and immediately returning to it to debrief and discuss it builds expectations in the readers' minds. They realize that the text is going to tell them something and that they need to, and eventually they will want to, think about what they are reading while they are reading it. Over time, often years, the reading, thinking, and discussing routine of transitional guided reading shifts a reader's expectation of the text so they anticipate what the text will provide. That shift is what makes students real readers.

During the step of returning to the text or the debriefing, teachers address study skills. Study skills are hands-on interactions with the text that improve comprehension. Study skills will be addressed in detail when we discuss transitional guided reading using nonfiction texts. Study skills tactics enable students to respond fully to the text. Responding is the last step of the teaching sequence.

Responding

The students have been prepared to read (been taken into the text), have read and discussed what they read (been taken through the text), and now they are ready to respond to the text (be taken beyond the text). Why do students need to respond at all? When we read for pleasure, we don't "do something" afterward like analyze the reading. Exactly; transitional guided reading is not preparation for pleasure reading, although (hopefully) reading will be pleasurable for the students. In reading instruction, students begin to learn to read like a writer and think about the reading while they are reading it.

In the past in most American schools, students traditionally completed workbook pages or work sheets after they read the story. It is still a common practice in many schools. As many teachers know, workbook pages and work sheets offer students a few decontextualized chances to fill in blanks, match items by drawing lines, mark certain situations, or complete some other simple action that requires minimal thought. Countless forests have been chopped down in the name of workbooks and work sheets. All to what end? No one ever became a better reader by filling in blanks.

In transitional guided reading, on the other hand, the book itself becomes a working book. Rather than send students to their seats with contrived work sheets, the teacher drives students back into the text by encouraging them to respond to the text by interacting with the concepts, skills, vocabulary, and writer's craft evident in the book. Responses are opportunities for expressing understanding. Blank papers of various sizes, adding machine tape, sticky notes, note cards, and even shelf paper are the hardware of responses. Usually, the artifacts in this teaching sequence can be graded.

Four types of responses allow students to deepen their understanding: oral, three dimensional, written, and image. Examples of each of type of response are described below.

Oral Responses

Rereading the text is the most obvious example of an oral response. Emergent and early readers benefit most from repeated readings of instructional texts during guided reading. This is not to say newly fluent readers can't improve by rereading texts. But why would a student reread a text? The students who are kings and queens of "I'm done!" will be difficult to convince to do anything again. So, what would convince them? Reading to a student in a lower grade, to senior citizens in a nearby nursing home, or to a visitor or reading into a mirror (vanity does have its virtue), reading into a karaoke machine, reading into a tape recorder, conducting a reader's theatre, reading aloud on video, and so on are all concrete ways to encourage a student to read and read again. Even practicing reading for a video or audio taping or practicing reading before an audience are authentic reasons to reread.

A class discussion itself counts as an oral response from students. Talking about a text soon after it was read helps students make diverse and immediate connections. Students learn to build on their ideas by using the ideas of others. They learn to explain, defend, argue, persuade, convince, and influence others through peaceful discussion. And, they learn that they can change their minds based on the ideas others offer. Discussions in transitional guided reading prepare students for the types of discussions that take place in reader's workshops, literature circles, book clubs, and life.

An oral presentation counts as an oral response. Students might report on a genre, author, book, or other topic. A "book talk" is an oral retelling of a book that includes summary and review. Book talks might involve artwork or props that also serve as visual and three-dimensional responses.

Three-Dimensional Responses

A three-dimensional response is a response that involves items that can be placed on a table. Nonfiction texts lend themselves more readily to three-dimensional responses than fiction texts. Traditionally, a three-dimensional response involved a shoe box, dollhouse furniture, and other odd materials that might be included in a diorama. It seems to me that nonfiction is a better place for a diorama.

A display or collection of items gathered by a student is a prime example of a three-dimensional response. In examples used in life science and earth science, seashells, seeds, leaves, rocks, bones, and other objects are organized by category or attribute and displayed on a table or shelf. A full-size object such as an uprooted sunflower, complete with dirt and roots, is another example. Birds' nests, abandoned wasp nests, beehives, honeycombs, and so on are others. Different types of pulleys, nuts, bolts, wires, springs, and other items used in physical science class can make fascinating collections and displays.

Displays require some kind of writing as well. Minimally, the display needs to have a title and caption. A placard that explains the source of the items and provides background information completes the display. Labels need to identify the various parts of an object. A map or globe pinpointing the location of the items provides additional information and yet another facet of dimensionality.

A narrative example of three-dimensional responses is a book-in-a-bag project. This response combines oral and three-dimensional responses. In preparing for such a response, a student collects various items that represent the characters, settings, and actions that make up the story. The items are gathered in a bag or box and used as props that illustrate the different points of an oral report. Afterward, a display might be constructed that includes the items and a copy of the book. Writing adds a third facet to the display. Labels or placards are written to identify each of the props. The display is titled, captioned, and often accompanied by a written summary or retelling of the book. Such a display requires more thinking and decision-making from students than a diorama and involves writing.

Written Responses

Typically, teachers think of a report, a huge undertaking, as the primary written response. As a matter of fact, many kinds of written responses give students practice in writing smaller amounts of text that may eventually help them write larger, longer written responses. Many of the examples of fiction written responses are appropriate for nonfiction. Each type of written response has its own structure.

A structure is an outline or framework that gives a piece of writing shape; it identifies the parts and places where the student should include the smaller sections of text that make up the piece of writing. A structure should not be confused with a formula. A formula is scarcely more than a fill-in-the-blank event. Formulas result in cloned responses. Structures allow the writer's own voice and style to come through. Written responses are used for both narrative and nonfiction texts.

Blurb

A blurb on the back of a book is often a reader's first hint about what's between the covers. A well-written blurb will entice readers without giving away all the good parts of the book. It offers the potential reader a preview or overview. Students can learn to write blurbs after they have finished reading a book. Blurbs, like other kinds of writing, have a structure. Blurbs might have four parts and run four to eight sentences long. Blurbs generally mention the content or story, the specific type of genre, and the author and the potential reader's feelings about the book. Each part might be one or two sentences long. All four parts of a blurb need not be included. Also, no rules apply about the appropriate order of these parts.

Summary

Summaries and blurbs are sometimes confused and writers often produce a hybrid of the two. Summaries and retellings are also often confused as the same kind of writing. However, each is its own entity with its own structure. We have already discussed the structure of a blurb. So, what is the difference between a summary and retelling? First of all, a summary is shorter and more general (rounder, if you will) than a retelling. Secondly, a summary may be completed at the end of a chapter or section or at the end of a whole book. A retelling, on the other hand, is generally written after the reader has finished all the reading.

A summary has three parts—the "who" (characters and setting in narrative texts; or the general subject in expository texts), the "what happened" (the action or plot in narrative texts; or the use of the object or process in expository texts), and the "so," which might include a conclusion, prediction, question, comparison, contrast, transition to a continuation, or other examples from the text. Each part of a summary is one or two sentences long. Some people include a fourth part as the first—an overall statement about the story's concept or genre. This information can be eased into the beginning and braided into the section that discusses the "who."

The "who" includes the names and positions or roles of the main character and mentions the setting. An example of a straight "who" beginning might sound like, "Crystal, one of the main characters, and her two friends are curious and smart. Other characters from their school and town try to take from the girls an odd rock they found." A summary that includes a mention of the concept might sound like this, "Crystal, one of the main character, and her two friends are curious and smart in this science fiction mystery. Other characters from their school, town, and government try to take from the girls an odd rock they found."

The "what happened" is a brief synopsis of the major action. The operative word here is "major." Students frequently have difficulty writing briefly at this point in the summary. Here is where the summary often becomes a retelling. A concise example sounds like, "The girls use the scientific method and lots of research to figure out where the rock comes from until a real scientist tells them the truth. Then, they have to decide what to do with it."

The "so" can be manifested in several ways, such as in a personal connection like a conclusion or prediction. For example, a conclusion might be something like, "I figured all along that the rock was from outer space." A prediction, which is included in a summary of a chapter or a few chapters, might sound like, "I'll bet we find out that the rock is from outer space" or, "I think the girls will sell the rock instead of giving it to the government." The last information included in a summary might be a question such as, "I wonder if there are any more of those rocks around?" or, "Who do you think should get the rock?" A quote from the text is sometimes the best summary; for example, "The hardest part for the three girls turned out to be figuring out what to do with the rock. Like Roxanne kept saying, 'Well, what do you guys think? What should we do with it?'" Occasionally, the last part of a summary might include a mention of some aspect of the writer's craft. For instance, students might include a reference to a stylistic device the author used, such as giving characters clever names. "The names of the characters really told what kind of people they were: the principal was Mrs. N. Charge and the newspaper reporter was Ms. Gabby Scribbler." By writing summaries, students learn to be brief yet explicit.

Retelling

There comes a time, however, when more is more. Retellings are longer, more detailed, and more sequential than summaries. The major difference between the two is the retelling's use of transitional words like "first," "then," "next," "soon," "later," "after that," "a while later," "and finally," "at the end," or "the story ended when . . ." Sequence can be indicated by other time references like "that morning," "after school," "in the spring," and so on. Eventually, students can be expected to use plot terms in their retellings, such as initiating action, rising action, crisis, resolution, and declining action to sequence the events. In general, the structure of a retelling includes a sequential replay of the events and the characters involved. The structure may follow the events chapter by chapter, episode by episode, or event by event. Sequence and completeness are the important considerations. The following is an example of a retelling.

The story begins when three friends, Crystal, Opal, and Roxanne, find a strange rock in a window box. The rock does many odd things like get hot, attract ceramics, and buzz. The girls decide to try and find out what the rock is and where it came from.

The next day they take the rock to school and two bullies, Josh and Cole, swipe it during recess. The playground aide takes it and gives it to the principal when a newspaper reporter happens to be visiting the school. The principal gives the rock back to the girls after school.

That night the girls use the scientific method to find out about the rock. They develop a hypothesis, check out books from the library, and search online. They find out a lot of information about rocks and they take notes. They figure out that the rock is probably from outer space since they couldn't find anything about what this rock can do. Now they have to decide what to do with it.

The next day there is an article in the paper and a television reporter is at the school. A colonel from the government, a museum lady, and a sleazy creep all want the rock. The girls keep the rock and try to find out more about it.

That afternoon, they take it to a rock show at the mall and ask a professor to help them. He does a lot of tests on the rock and tells them it is from outer space. At the end, the girls decide to give it to the government so scientists can study it. Crystal, Opal, and Roxanne name the rock. They call it Bensonite after the name of their town. The story ends with Roxanne finding another rock in a planter.

Review Statements

A short, quick written response is a review statement. Students tend to enjoy writing review statements because they are short and the students get to write what they think about what they have read. As an affective response, review statements allow students to offer personal expressions of like or dislike. Students can be introduced to review statements by reviewing samples inside the front matter of books. Generally, only good reviews are included in published works. However, students need to realize that a review does not have to be favorable. Reviews are critiques. Critiques discuss both the good and the ugly qualities of a book. Here is where children learn to be mindful and thoughtful when having to deliver less-than-satisfactory news.

Review statements are one or two sentences long. They do not necessarily need to include full sentences. The review statements might reference the story itself, the genre, the author, and, of course, the reader's feelings about the story, genre, or author. Some examples are offered here:

"This is another story by one of my favorite authors. It is funny with weird characters and silly action."

"I couldn't stop thinking of people I knew as I read this book."

"If you like bugs and other kinds of creepy things, you will love this story. I sure did."

"This story was too long. I think the author could have cut out all the jibber jabber about being a good person."

"I don't know why I started this book. I don't even like horses."

One school media center I visited displayed the jackets of several popular books pinned up on a bulletin board. Student review statements were written on strips of adding machine tape and pinned up around the particular jacket of the reviewed book. Each review was signed with the student's name, grade, and room number. Several of the books reviewed were displayed on a shelf near the bulletin board for students to borrow, read, and offer their take on. This display helps student understand that they are engaged in meaningful reading and meaningful writing for meaningful purposes.

As with learning any kind of writing, learning the structure of a response and finding a voice for the response takes time and effort. Students can prepare for writing review statements by offering verbal reviews of events throughout the day. They might practice writing short reviews of the book the teacher reads aloud each day. They might write a review of a fellow student's writing or give an oral report about a school concert, school play, television episode, or the morning announcements—whatever. The more writing students can complete within a structure, the better they get at writing in that format.

Explanations

Explanations are written just as frequently in response to narrative texts as expository texts. Explanations are generally a paragraph that discusses the function or purpose of a book. In other words, they clarify how or why a character acted in some way or how or why a process works. Narrative explanations often deal with motivation; why a character did what he or she did. Expository explanations may deal with cause and effect.

The structure uses a typical paragraph form. The topic sentence introduces the function, purpose, or process being explained. The body of the paragraph includes details organized sequentially that include ordinal words such as "first," "then," "next," "after that," and "finally." Explanations may include examples or situations from the book and they generally end with a conclusion.

Descriptions

Descriptions are often confused with explanations. Descriptions involve sensory attributes. Attributes might include visual elements such as dimensions and colors or other elements such as sounds, scents, or textures. Narrative descriptions may deal with character traits or indicators.

Traits are obvious; they tell the reader the character was seven feet tall, for example. Indicators show, as in, "He stooped to enter the doorway." Better writers use character indicators because they show rather than tell. Readers tend to enjoy indicators more because they are able to make more personal connections or more personal interpretations about what the writer provided. A narrative description may concern affective attributes as well. These deal with how characters feel or cause other characters to feel.

Descriptions may include dimensions of setting. Setting includes so much more information than the place where an event happened. Settings include time—time of day or year, time measured in eons, and time in the life of the character. Weather is another dimension of setting. Multifactored descriptions add dimensionality to the setting. Often descriptions and narrative events complement each other and may appear together.

Thought Bubbles

Thought bubbles are almost exclusively used in narrative responses. Reading instruction is all about the thinking. Nothing gets readers thinking like asking them to decide what the characters are thinking. Thought bubbles involve inference, a fairly high level thinking skill. Students write down what the character is thinking within the context of the situation. Transitional guided reading books are perfect for thought bubbles because they are longer picture books.

After students have read and discussed a chapter, ask them to choose a character in an illustration. Two-by-two-inch sticky notes are perfect for this task. Show the students how to make a thought bubble shape on the writing side of the sticky. Demonstrate how to place the sticky above the character's head—with the corner containing an anchor bubble pointing to (or touching) the character's head. The character does not have to be a major character; passersby, other uninvolved people, or even animals can be given thinking bubbles. Sometimes these make for the most interesting writing.

The students need to determine what the character is thinking based on what is happening in the story. Most children attempt this task with ease and write the thought bubble in a first person voice as the character. Other children have a difficult time using a first person voice for a character and write in the second person. Over time, those children learn to write in thought bubbles just fine.

Questions

Certainly the text, no matter if it is narrative or expository, does not answer all questions about the situation or process a student might ask. Students need to learn to inquire more of the text and author. Asking questions is a sign of curiosity. Students need to learn what to ask about and how to ask it. They also need to learn to avoid the traps of the yes or no question and the literal question.

Questions generally involve who, what, when, where, why, and how. Other questions include such words as "are," "will," "was," "were," "can," "could," "would," "should," "might," "do," "does," "did," and others. The ways these words are joined with other words determine the degree of the question's insight and value. Stems are the front half of a statement or question that can be finished for different purposes. For example, who, what, when, and where can be combined with a number of verbs to construct various question stems. Consider these combinations:

Who/What/When/Where is ____?

Who/What/When/Where are ____?

Who/What/When/Where was ____?

Who/What/When/Where were ____?

Who/What/When/Where will ____?

Who/What/When/Where does ____?

Who/What/When/Where did ____?

These represent literal level questions. The answers are right there in the text. The questions do not require that the students engage in a great deal of thought beyond finding the answer and should factor minimally in questioning and question writing. Likewise, questions to which the answer is "yes" or "no" should be avoided as much as possible because they lead to no higher thinking. For example,

Can a/the/this/it/you/we/she/he/they ____?

Could a/the/this/it/you/we/she/he/they ____?

Should a/the/this/it/you/we/she/he/they ____?

Would a/the/this/it/you/we/she/he/they ____?

Will a/the/this/it/you/we/she/he/they ____?

Did a/the/this/it/you/we/she/he/they ____?

Does a/the/this/it/she/he ____?

Do the/you/we/they ____?

Have you ever ____?

Is it possible to ____?

On the other hand, consider these combinations:

Who/What/When/Where can ____?

Who/What/When/Where could ____?

Who/What/When/Where should ____?

Who/What/When/Where would ____?

Who/What/When/Where might ____?

Who/What/When/Where do you think ____?

Who/What/When/Where does this remind you of?

What type of person/place ____?

What ways
were/are/will/could/would/should/can/did/do/
might ____?

What
is/are/were/will/could/would/should/can/did/do/did/
might ____?

What happens when/if ____?

What if ____?

What is a reason for/to ____?

What would happen if ____?

Why
is/are/were/will/could/would/should/can/did/do/did/
might ____?

How
is/are/were/will/could/would/should/can/did/do/did/
might ____?

How in the world ____?

Why in the world ____?

These questions are two layers thick. They require the reader to delve into the reader's schema, and, at the same time, they require the student to establish a rationale and engage in deeper thought.

If only. "If" is such a small word, yet it is a great question starter. It stirs readers' thinking and encourages them to conjure up possibilities. Consider these:

If it was possible ____?

If you/we/he/she/they/anyone/someone/no one could ____?

If there was/were/is/are ____?

If ever ____?

Indeed, if only.

Questions, multilayered questions, enable students to investigate, consider alternatives, probe, and examine what might be possible. Questioning is all about the thinking.

Key Words

A major way that nonfiction responses differ from fiction responses is the way key words factor so prominently into nonfiction written responses.

Key words are the most important words in a section heading, sentence, paragraph, page, or section. These include the content vocabulary, those words directly related to the concept or content. Key words may be set off by bold print, italicized, or marked with a color overlay that looks like highlighting tape. Key words may be individual words or phrases. These words often appear in indexes or glossaries. Students need to learn how to determine which words are the key words. They can write the words on sticky notes, on note cards, or in a notebook. Wherever any information is copied from a book, the page on which it appears needs to be noted as well.

Notes

In general, nonfiction written responses involve some kind of note taking. Note taking gives students practice writing words or phrases, practice that may help them understand that copying directly from the book is a bad idea—not just because writing out long passages is too much work, but of course because it is illegal. Note taking is a part of a student's set of study skills. Study skills were investigated in detail in chapter 4. As we discussed earlier, note taking is the second tactic in study skills use. Students learn note taking during transitional guided reading lessons that return to the text, during the debriefing. Opportunities for taking notes are more obvious and frequent in nonfiction texts.

Frequently the hardest part of taking notes is knowing what to write. Students often face the temptation to copy everything from the book. Short and sweet notes are what teachers and students want to record. Students need to learn that notes are bits of information, not complete sentences—a word or phrase is plenty. Students need to locate and record content vocabulary, or key words, and the corresponding page numbers on which the information appears. If the word is defined or explained in the text, the student should record a brief version of that definition. Using symbols often saves time in note taking. For example, an equal sign serves as a symbol for "means" or "is an example of." A whole definition need not be written. A shorter synonym for a word works as well. Other symbols such as the not-equal sign, arrowhead, ellipsis, colon, and so on can all be used to stand in the place of words.

Facts such as dates and proper nouns serve as fodder for note taking. This is not to say that notes cannot be taken while reading fiction. Features of a writer's craft such as the execution of the literary elements and stylistic devices are examples of information that might be recorded in narrative note taking. As described earlier, character traits and indicators can be noted, as can evidence of settings.

Notes are taken about each paragraph in transitional guided reading. In preparing students for more complicated types of nonfiction writing, like the report, it is important that students practice skills that prevent them from copying texts. Key information, such as words and phrases, are copied on to sticky notes, on to note cards, or in a notebook. Using a bulleted list, rather than a numeric or lettered list, prevents students from thinking of the information in a hierarchy form and provides opportunities for students to cluster and organize their information later (the fourth tactic in study skills use).

In addition, students will retrieve that information to verify, clarify, and extend it (the third study skills tactic). Since the information will be revisited and eventually moved around, students need to code the corners of their sticky note or note cards with page and paragraph numbers. Generally the page number is placed in the lower left-hand corner and the paragraph symbol and number is placed in the lower right-hand corner. Placing this information on the lower edge of the sticky note, the edge opposite the sticky edge, orients the sticky note so it can be used for note taking. The information can be recorded on the sticky note before it is placed in the margin beside each paragraph so the surface hangs off the page.

The same annotations of page and paragraph numbers can be done on note cards. Banding the cards together or putting them in an envelope or card box keeps them together. Notes written in a notebook require page and paragraph information as well.

Professional writers always cite or acknowledge their sources. Students eventually will be expected to cite their sources when this writing skill becomes a measured grade level standard. Information gathered from several sources might be organized by color; students can code the source using variations on the colors of sticky notes or note cards. Separate sections of a notebook can be dedicated to separate sources of information. Generally, an individual district or building identifies the preferred style of annotating sources of information. A consistent style should be maintained through the grades if automaticity is expected to be attained.

Index

An index is one type of expository or access feature some nonfiction books contain. It is an alphabetical listing of key words contained in the text accompanied by the page numbers on which each word appears.

If a nonfiction book does not have an index, a student can make one. Students can gather key words and the page numbers on which the words appear during note taking. These words can then be alphabetized and listed with the page numbers. Unlike a publisher's index, an index made by students will include only the page number on which the word first appears.

Glossary

A glossary is another kind of expository feature included in some nonfiction books. It is an alphabetical list of some key words and their definitions. Some glossaries include pronunciation guides as well. Nonfiction books may have a glossary and no index; some may have an index and no glossary. Not all of the words from an index are included in a glossary. However, if a word appears in the glossary, it should appear in the index. A glossary generally contains words that are not commonly understood or those that are not already defined or explained in the body of the text.

As with an index, if a glossary is not included by the publisher, one can be made. Students can use their key words notes to determine which words are commonly understood and which are not. Using the page number recorded for the not commonly known words, they skim the page looking for definitions or explanations.

Students sort through the unknown words to determine which should be included in the glossary. Some words that are defined in the body may need to be explained in simpler terms in the glossary. A two-by-four-inch sticky note is just the right size for writing down a word and its definition or explanation. Using individual sticky notes for individual words provides the needed flexibility when alphabetizing.

Footnotes and Sidebars

Key words may be defined or explained on the page they first appear in a footnote or sidebar. A footnote is a sentence or two written in a smaller font positioned in the bottom margin of the page that provides further information about a term or idea; a sidebar provides similar information but is written in the outer margin. In addition, footnotes or sidebars can be used to provide examples, references, or related information. An asterisk or other kind of symbol should be inserted in the text at the point of application. The same symbol needs to be used to lead the reader to the additional information. Students can attach the additional information to the margins using adding machine tape and temporary glue or two-by-four-inch sticky notes.

Captions

Captions are a type of expository or access feature some nonfiction books contain. They are almost exclusively written responses to nonfiction texts. Captions have two purposes: to describe what is seen or to explain what is happening in an image. These descriptions and explanations are called captions when they accompany a map, figure, photograph, or illustration. They are called summary statements when associated with a table, graph, or other kind of graphic organizer that displays quantitative information. Do not ask the students to decide whether to use a caption or summary statement. This distinction doesn't really matter in the big picture.

Captions and summary statements are generally one or two sentences. A well-written caption for a well-chosen image usually includes relevant key words from the text. However, the caption should not duplicate a sentence directly from the text. Students can write captions on two-by-four-inch sticky notes or on strips of adding machine tape adhered to the image with a swipe of paste from a temporary glue stick. Like other kinds of written responses, once students learn how to write them, captions can be completed as homework or seat work. And, like other types of written responses, captions produce an artifact whose quality can be measured and used to determine a student's grade.

Labels

Labels are key words or phrases that identify the specific parts that make up a figure. Since labels are not full sentences, they generally do not require uppercase letters or punctuation. Using arrows or lines to connect key words to specific places or items is always a good idea. Generally, a caption describes or explains the image as a whole. In addition, the figure may have a heading or title.

Titles and Headings

Narrative texts have chapters; nonfiction or expository texts have sections. The organizational difference between these texts concerns access and consumption. Chapters are like beads on a string—they need to be accessed one at a time and in order; otherwise, the text will seem like a confusing mess. Sections, on the other hand, can be imagined like the sections of an orange. Any section can be read first, they do not need to be accessed in order, readers do not have to consume them all at once, and the whole thing can be shared. When a segment has been read, each student in the group might come up with a title for that segment. Students will most likely need direct teaching and guided practice to determine the most appropriate title for a section, chapter, or image. The title is written on the sticky note.

Chapter or section titles and other types of headings are synthesis statements, which require a high level thinking skill. Writing titles gives students practice synthesizing the essential information in a segment of text into as few words as possible, usually not more than five words. Titles are not full sentences; they are statements. This process helps students understand the power inherent in a well-constructed fragment.

Chapter titles generally center on one of the literary elements of character, setting, or action. Section titles usually center on the main idea of the segment and include key words. Segments of sections in nonfiction texts may be identified by titles. Images, figures, and graphic organizers need titles as well. Like other titles, the titles for these images concern the main idea and include key words. In this way, students learn to categorize and synthesize information. Writing titles and headings helps students determine the sequence and hierarchy of information delivery. The list of titles the students create may serve as an outline of the material covered in the chapter.

Table of Contents

A table of contents is another type of expository or access feature included in some nonfiction texts. A table of contents indicates the range and organizational scheme of the key concepts contained in a nonfiction book. In fiction, it offers the sequence of plot development. As students determine titles for chapters or sections in transitional guided reading, they might include the range of page numbers for each as well. When they have completed reading the book, the students might design a table of contents for it using paper cut to the book's trim size. The titles, dotted lines, and page numbers are organized and centered on the page, along with an illustration or design to complement the rest of the book.

A student-made table of contents.

Outlines

Were you the type of student who wrote the report and *then* did the outline? I know I couldn't have been the only one. When should outlining begin? Well, in the context of those five phases of human learning, awareness begins as early as first grade, direct teaching begins in grade two, and then guided practice begins in grades three through four, with independent practice beginning in grade five. If students begin to develop an awareness of what will be taught next, the subsequent learning seems more natural.

A table of contents is a precursor to an outline. In truth, a table of contents *is* an outline. Outlining 101 takes place every time students and their teachers investigate or write a table of contents. Students can learn about the features and structure of an outline by examining the titles, headings, and subheadings that make up the framework of an expository text. The titles that already appear in the book can serve as the scaffolding for note taking in a notebook. Headings are main ideas; key words and phrases are the details.

Image Responses

Any kind of graphic representation of text information, whether expository or narrative, counts as an image response. Image responses are vehicles for expressing understanding, just as oral, written, or three-dimensional responses are. Student comprehension involves determining what type of image response best suits a particular task. The types of graphic organizers are so diverse they can't be counted—timeline, cycle, schematic grid, Venn diagram, herringbone, plot map, storyboard, or even a plain old picture.

Illustrations

Traditionally, an image response referred to an illustration. Images are more than pictures, however. As a patron of the arts, I have no problem with students drawing in response to reading. But let's be honest, we all know that too often students draw to avoid reading or doing other kinds of literacy work. Drawing in response to reading needs to include specific information that represents many dimensions of the reading and provides ample opportunities for the students to express the depth of their understanding.

Illustrations in response to narrative text should include evidence of the book's literary elements, including character, setting, and plot. Plenty of accurate details specific to the text should be apparent. Interpreting the writer's words is a part of comprehending those words. Including speeches or thought bubbles provides an added dimension. Minimally, the illustration should have a title and caption. A written summary completes the response.

Illustrations in response to expository texts should include complete, accurate details about the information in the book. Precision is the key to reproducing nonfiction information. Each part of the illustration should be labeled. A title, caption, and summary add important layers of information.

Graphic Representations

Nonfiction texts obviously lend themselves to graphic organization because of the kind of information covered in them. Books of black line masters and various kinds of graphic organizers fill the shelves of teacher supply stores. While these resources offer plenty of ideas, I caution against using them as worksheets. We all know that one size does not fit even most students anymore. The same is true when a template (black line master) is used generically. In other words, too often the information students need to record does not fit the blanks on a handout. If students have more information than can be included in the space the master provides, they may face doubt as to the accuracy of their selection of information and choose to eliminate some details in order to make the information fit. Or, students may have less information and suspect they need more and add unrelated or erroneous information just to make it fit. Students can design their own organizers using samples and direct teaching. Being responsible for designing their own graphic organizers shifts greater responsibility to the learners and engages them in various layers of thinking.

Graphic organizers visually depict text information. The type of information being represented determines the shape of the organizer. In other words, when two aspects of a concept are considered together, the image needs to have two planes. Compare and contrast or cause and effect analyses have two aspects and so need two areas. Two-ring Venn diagrams, T-graphs, and herringbone (fish bone) diagrams are appropriate methods of displaying these types of information. Timelines, cycles, and storyboards show sequences of events or the passage of time. A schematic grid displays several items according to their attributes, characteristics, or traits.

These tools will help students engage in more thoughtful and thorough learning experiences during transitional reading time. Now that we've covered all the components that aid comprehension, we'll examine how to make these elements work together in reader's workshops.

Part IV

Putting It All Together

6

Reader's Workshop

This practice evolves from transitional guided reading. Similarities exist between the setup of the two practices, but the responsibilities of reading and debriefing shift during reader's workshops. A reader's workshop is the first practice in which students read away from the group. It uses fiction exclusively. It is the most teacher-directed of all the instructional practices for truly fluent readers. The teacher is responsible for every aspect of the process.

First, the teacher forms a group of five to seven truly fluent readers. The group members might be assembled together because they share a common interest in the topic, genre, or author of a book. The group might be assembled due to curricular needs.

Next, the teacher selects a text appropriate for that group. Narrative instructional texts need to be 90 to 95 percent familiar to the members of the group. The details of familiarity were described in chapter 4. The text should be a not-too-long chapter book. The Fountas and Pinnell levels of books appropriate for reader's workshop range from O through S. The teacher must read the book before deciding to use it.

The teacher needs to determine where to break the book into readable and discussable segments. Segments may be as long as a chapter or longer; that is, the teacher must select sensible places to stop and discuss the text. A second consideration in breaking the book into pieces is the time needed to process each segment. Each reader's workshop lesson involves reading and completing a task independent of the group; then debriefing the task, discussing the reading, conducting the next minilesson, and explaining the next segment and task in the group. The teacher needs to establish a time line for each facet of that work.

Once the teacher decides on the length of segments, the teacher needs to identify the teaching point in each segment. The minilesson might introduce, teach, or review a concept, skill, or vocabulary word. This lesson is still instructive, so explicit information needs to be taught and learned; hence the term "minilesson." The teaching point generally covers some objective from the curriculum. These may include concepts, literacy or comprehension skills, or vocabulary words. Because truly fluent readers read like writers, students will devote a great deal of attention to the writer's craft. Chapter books selected for use in reader's workshop lessons should be rich and multidimensional with possibilities for examining the author's choices and techniques. The teacher needs to select and make note of what concepts will be attended to in each segment and how to teach those concepts. It is important to remember that the minilesson is mini—generally fewer than five minutes. The minilesson needs to be explicit, narrow, focused, and drawn from information in the segment.

While the teacher prepares the minilesson, he or she needs to determine the kinds of tasks students will complete during or just after they read the segment. The teacher directs students in a task that enables them to interact with the information taught during the minilesson. The task is directly related to the concept, skill, vocabulary word, or aspect of craft introduced in the minilesson. The task drives the children back into the text to revisit and interact with the concepts, skills, and vocabulary words the text offers. The children return to the text to practice using the teaching points from the minilesson. They express their understanding with oral, written, or image responses. These tasks generally involve marking the text with highlighter tape or edge tabs, completing some kind of short writing assignment, such as a list or paragraph, or creating an image, such as a Venn diagram or time line. Reading the text enables students to recognize what was taught in context; the task enables them to indicate their level of understanding and their ability to apply a concept via an artifact.

Teaching Sequence

Book Introduction

The first day with a new book involves certain discussion elements that are only incorporated on the first day. Sometimes the first lesson with a book includes only an introduction, without asking the students to begin to read the text. Before the book is even given to the students, the teacher tells the students what the book is about. In other words, the teacher introduces the main idea of the entire story. This provides an immediate schema for the students to match when they begin reading. The book will have schema relevance if the book is 90 to 95 percent familiar to the members of the group. The genre and motifs are discussed. The teacher talks about details of the author's life, work, style, and so on. If the author is familiar to the students, other works and style elements are discussed. The teacher gives each student a copy of the book after these aspects of the conversation are completed.

The conversation continues and covers the title and cover illustration. The back cover is often overlooked in reading instruction, even though it is a major source of information for adult and proficient student readers. The back cover may include a blurb or review statements. These may be read aloud by the teacher or individual students and then discussed. The conversation about the front and back covers should not be rushed, but the teacher should resist the temptation to linger over and exhaust every single aspect of the cover.

The group then moves into the book. Students often ignore front matter, which may include an introduction, preface, or foreword. The group lesson is a situation in which students learn the value of these parts. The students might read these silently in the group and then discuss them; or individuals might read a paragraph aloud and discuss its elements.

The table of contents highlights the organizational scheme of the book's sequence. Chapter length may indicate plot points. By the time students are truly fluent, they should be adept at recognizing the last page of each chapter and determining the length of each chapter. Chapter titles generally reference the literary elements of character, setting, or action. The conversation about the table of contents may include some student predictions. Students need resources about the book in order to make a prediction. Lack of sufficient information only encourages students to guess. At this point in the discussion, students have enough information to make predictions—the concept, genre, blurb, review statements, and perhaps biographical information about the author all provide fodder for the student to use when making a prediction.

Setting the Scene

The first step in any instructional encounter is setting the scene. This step is a part of the awareness phase of learning. The teacher gives students an indication of what they will be reading. Without giving away any important plot points, the teacher alludes to aspects of plot, character, and style evident in the coming segment.

Minilesson

The minilesson may introduce, review, or apply a vocabulary word, skill, or concept. It involves direct teaching and a degree of guided practice by the teacher. The teacher has already determined the teaching point for the segment.

The minilesson generally begins with the teacher telling the students what they are going to learn about—the concept, skill, vocabulary, or aspect of craft. The students might even write this topic or concept in a notebook. Then the teacher defines or explains what the concept is, an explanation the students might also write in their notebook. The teacher points out an example or two within the segment to be read; the students also record this. For example, Ivy Ruckman, author of *Night of the Twisters*, wrote the main character Dan Hatcher with a distinct voice. Part of his voice comes from the use of rhetorical questions. The use of rhetorical questions as a stylistic devise is a typical concept covered in a minilesson.

The teacher tells the students they are going to learn about a literary device authors use to give characters a distinct voice. (Of course, the students may already know about voice. Or, if not, the teacher can use this lesson to introduce voice as the teaching point.) The teacher might then discuss voice with the students, including plenty of rhetorical questions to facilitate student awareness. The teacher then explains exactly what rhetorical questions are—questions people ask but don't expect others to answer, questions that don't require an answer. The teacher also explains that some people pepper their conversations with rhetorical questions and don't even realize it; this behavior is a type of character indicator, something that an author has a character exhibit to show what kind of person he or she is. The teacher then directs the students to an example or two in the text. Such places in the text need to be located and marked prior to the lesson. Minilessons deal with one or two teaching points at a time.

Writing using a first person voice is a second teaching point Ruckman offers in this text. The teacher tells students that this story is written in first person and teaches the markers of a first person narrative: I, me, my, mine, and myself. The teacher then tells a quick story in the first person, counting off the markers. As the next step, students should find the markers in the text and record them.

The Task

The tasks students must complete are independent practices that help push students further along the learning curve. They produce artifacts that the teacher can use to determine how well the students have learned what has been taught. To produce artifacts for the minilessons described above, students might make a list of every rhetorical question used in the segment. Likewise, they might record each first-person marker word on a sheet of paper folded in columns. Whenever students copy anything from a source, they need to record the page and paragraph numbers at the same time. Students' ability to complete these tasks determines the degree to which they are able to recognize rhetorical questions and first person narrative markers. If this task goes well, a further task might include asking students to write a first person narrative paragraph that includes at least one rhetorical question.

After the students understand what to read, the minilesson has been executed, the students know what is involved in completing the task, and the group members know when they will meet next—all of which takes about twenty to twenty-five minutes—off the students go to read, think, and work. The teacher calls the next group and so it goes.

Reading the Text

The members of the group disembark to complete their array of work: seat work, center work, reading work, and tasks. They read independently at their own pace, knowing that both the reading and the task need to be completed before the next group meeting. Truly fluent students may want to read near each other but do not often want to read aloud to each other. However, it is up to the teacher to make those kinds of decisions. The teacher may dedicate classroom time for the students to read, or the students may read on the bus, at home, in study hall, or wherever. The teacher may also offer class time to complete the tasks. Again, it is up to the teacher to decide if the students should work together or alone.

Returning to the Text

At a predetermined time, usually a day or two after the previous meeting, the group meets, each member having read the segment and completed the task. They should approach the table with book tabbed and work in hand. The return to the text has two facets—discussing the reading and debriefing the task.

The teacher orchestrates the next segment of reading, conducts the next minilesson, directs the task, and the students go off to read. This five-step routine continues throughout the reading. The steps of reader's workshop routine include:

Week One

Monday   Group meets and teacher sets the scene for entire book.
            Teacher introduces the book.
Tuesday   Group meets and teacher establishes the length of segment
            and due date for the reading and the task.
            Teacher sets the scene for first segment.
            Teacher conducts the minilesson.
            Teacher explains the first task.
Wednesday   Students read first segment independently.
            Students complete the first task independently.
Thursday   Group meets with teacher and discusses the first segment.
            Group and teacher debrief the first task.
            Teacher establishes the length of second segment and due
            date for the reading and the task.
            Teacher sets the scene for second segment.
            Teacher conducts the minilesson.
            Teacher explains the second task.
Friday   Catch-up day for teacher and students to complete
            unfinished tasks.

Week Two

Monday   Group meets with teacher and discusses the second
            segment.
            Group and teacher debrief the second task.
            Teacher establishes the length of third segment and due
            date for the reading and the task.
            Teacher sets the scene for third segment.
            Teacher conducts the minilesson.
            Teacher explains the third task.
Tuesday   Students read third segment independently.
            Students complete the third task independently.
Wednesday   Group meets and the routine continues.

By establishing a plan to conduct effective reader's workshops, teachers help students enhance their comprehension skills while they learn to work independent from the group.

Literature circles are explored in the next chapter, which discusses how each student focuses on a specific aspect of a book and then shares this information in a reading group to deepen every student's understanding of each book.

Literature Circles

The next instructional practice picks up where reader's workshops leave off. In literature circles, students continue to learn about reading and analyzing the author's craft. This instructional practice continues to shift greater and more explicit types of responsibility to the readers. It streamlines student thinking by asking each member of the group to read for specific aspects of the text. Each student learns the responsibilities of the assigned role and refines his or her interpretation of the text and the writer's craft. Different people are given different roles in a literature circle. In general, the roles center on the literary elements of character, setting, and action, as well as on the writer's craft. Some examples include:

- Character Captain
- Scene Setter
- Vocabulary Master
- Passage Picker
- Connector
- Researcher
- Artful Artist

The original concept of literature circles was developed by Harvey Daniels to help ensure that students glean all that literature has to offer. The principle that underscores literature circles holds that literature is best understood when a group of students investigate the many facets of a story and then pool understandings.

A literature circle involves a conversation between teachers and students, and ultimately between students, about a chapter book or novel. Participants assume one of several roles. Each role requires that students take notes while reading so they are prepared to take part in a discussion. Each student approaches the text from a slightly different angle and with a slightly different purpose. The members of a group read a common text independently, each with a particular focus in mind. The group then meets to discuss what they have read and they work together to build a collective understanding of the concept of the book. The ultimate goal of literature circles is to enable students to think deeply about a book without teacher supervision.

Groupings and Books

Literature circles are conducted with groups of six or seven truly fluent members who read at a similar level. The groups may be formed according to student interest, genre, or author, or teaching point. A class might have a number of combinations of groups at any one time. For example, one classroom may have one literature circle group, a reciprocal teaching group, and two transitional guided reading groups.

On the other hand, a class might have two or three literature circles going on simultaneously, each group reading a different novel. The groups may be reading books by the same author or within the same genre; or not. If similar types of books are being read, the groups read, collect information, and then compile what they have learned to generate a detailed understanding of the author or genre. The group members accept different roles each time the group meets so they are able to read and think from different points of view.

Books for literature circles are longer chapter books or novels. Keep in mind that the longer the book, the longer it will take the students to finish it. Teachers are leading group discussions after each segment, don't forget. It is not important that students dedicate weeks or months to a single tome. It is important that students read different kinds of literature while still under the knowledgeable, watchful eyes of the teacher. Students engaged in literature circles continue to learn about reading at this stage of development. They are being shaped as future consumers of quality texts. They are learning to recognize what makes writing good and what good writing does for the reader.

A literature circle is an instructional practice. Instruction is generally tied to objectives, which are tied to standards. So, the teacher is responsible for making instructional decisions, including deciding what materials are to be used. To this end, the teacher needs to select the book to be read. Later on, the teacher might gather an array of books that reflect the current objectives or standards that need to be learned. Groups might then select from the array.

Training

Phase I

Students learn their roles and responsibilities during phase I. The teacher assigns the students to the different roles, initiates each responsibility, and establishes the routine of literature circles. Using a simple text that is perhaps three or four levels lower than the group's narrative instructional level during the training period ensures that students are free to focus on their roles and responsibilities as they learn to prepare and participate in literature circles.

The teacher trains all the members of the group in one role at a time during phase I. That is, each member learns how to be the character captain at the same time. Every student with this responsibility learns what to recognize while reading, how to mark the examples, what techniques to use when taking notes, and how to participate in the discussion. Two or three days may be needed to adequately train students about the expectations of their role. Essentially, it may take two weeks or more to train students in their roles and responsibilities. Taking the time up front to fully train students is time well spent in the long run.

During the first lessons of phase I, the teacher determines the length of the segment to be read and teaches students about the sort of information they should attend to in the role. The students learn how to record information using recording forms and how to apply other types of note-taking skills. Harvey Daniels has designed specific recording sheets for each of the roles. These are available in his book *Literature Circles: Voice and Choice in Book Clubs & Reading Groups* (Stenhouse Publishers, 2001). During the training phase, the teacher offers guided practice as the students read and record information. When finished, the teacher and students discuss what they have learned.

Each member of the group might use a notebook to record information while reading within their role. Students can add information other members of the group bring up during the group's discussion in the notebook. The notebook serves as a literary log of works read, analyzed, and discussed. It becomes an artifact that can be evaluated to determine student grades and displayed as evidence of student performance at parent conferences.

Students will begin to comment on each other's conclusions and question each other during the discussion as their reading, thinking, and discussing skills improve. Eventually, roles begin to disappear and students begin to participate in discussions in somewhat sophisticated, knowledgeable terms. The goal of instruction is to take students to a point where the roles no longer matter; students just read and discuss.

Roles

The members of a literature circle participate in the group discussion according to the responsibilities associated with their roles. Their responsibilities focus the reader's attention on certain literary elements and aspects of the writer's craft. This information is discussed in detail in chapter 9. The information the students provide becomes the discussion points. Each time a member makes a point, he or she must direct the other members to a place in the text that illustrates the point. At first, students need to learn not to interfere with the responsibilities of other roles. After each member shares what he or she noted, the discussion director asks if any students have anything to add or say. Eventually, however, the roles will erode and students will just discuss the whole text. Let's examine some of the roles and responsibilities in literature circles.

Discussion Director

This is the premier job in the circle because it is basically the boss of the group. This individual makes sure all the members of the group are present and prepared. The director initiates the discussion with a comment or two about what he or she thinks about the segment and asks the other members what they think. The director orchestrates the discussion by identifying who speaks next.

Character Captain

The student in this role explores the literary element of characters. The student focuses on and takes notes about main characters, minor characters, antagonists, and protagonists. He or she makes a bulleted list of character traits and character indicators. This student records and discusses how a character develops over the course of a text and how different characters interact. The character captain may also make notes and express personal feelings about a character or make predictions about the rest of the book.

Scene Setter

Attending to another literary element, this person takes notes about the dimensions of setting, including and beyond place. This student focuses on details such as the book's time of day, week, and month; time measured by eons; and seasons and weather. The student also discusses the ways those details affect the action and characters. The student in this role relays how the scene has shifted from the previous segment.

Vocabulary Master

This individual records vocabulary words he or she thinks members of the group need to understand. The student copies words or phrases and the page numbers on which they appear. The vocabulary master first records what he or she thinks the meaning of the word is from the context. Then the student finds the meanings by consulting a thesaurus, dictionary, or another person and shares the meanings with the group during the discussion.

Passage Picker

The student in this role explores the writer's craft. Particularly beautiful or funny turns of phrase are found and recorded with page number. Examples include similes, metaphors, and imagery. Segments of dialogue might be included as well. The passage picker explains why he or she found those passages interesting.

Connector

The student in this role explores literary elements as well as the writer's craft. This member connects characters, settings, and actions to other characters, settings, or actions in other books, movies, or television shows or in his or her own life for the purpose of comparing or contrasting. Elements of the author's style are also connected to those of other authors.

Researcher

The student in this role steps over into another content area. This person investigates background information on some aspect of the story. For example, if the story takes place in France, this person studies France and offers information about French culture or history. Or, if one character is a private investigator, the researcher might find out how a person becomes a private investigator. If the story takes place during the Civil War, the student gathers information about that period and shares it with the group.

Artful Artist

Another favorite role, the student in this role illustrates the segment. The illustration needs to include evidence of each literary element. The illustrations might be done on half sheets of paper and compiled into a storyboard complete with titles and captions. The illustrator discusses what inspired the interpretation with specific references to the text.

Phase II

In phase I the teacher introduces the group to the book by setting the scene for the entire book in a way that is similar to what is done in reader's workshop. The teacher assigns roles, determines the length of the first segment, and sets up the next time the group will meet and discuss the text. Students generally have two or three days to complete the reading and note taking. The students read independently, take notes, and prepare for the discussion.

The members meet at the appointed time with books and notes in hand. The discussion director starts them off and the discussion begins. The group determines the length of the next segment and the next meeting date. Literature circles usually meet twice a week.

Initially, the teacher remains a member of the group, but a member who participates less and less. He or she serves as a coach who eventually backs off completely. Over time, the children are able to completely orchestrate the reading and run the discussion. Thus begins phase II of literature circles.

Groups of truly fluent readers learn how to conduct a literature circle and then learn how to conduct reciprocal teaching. Students might alternate between the two types of practice, taking part in a literature circle about a narrative text then engaging in reciprocal teaching with an expository text.

The next chapter details how teachers can help students explore a nonfiction text using various aspects of shared experience.

8

Reciprocal Teaching

This instructional practice for truly fluent readers is a cousin of literature circles because both practices involve students by giving them roles with responsibilities that focus their thinking. Reciprocal teaching is used with nonfiction texts, while a literature circle is used with fiction. The reciprocal teaching method was developed by Ann Marie Palincsar to help high school students read and understand their science and social studies textbooks. Like literature circles, reciprocal teaching is used to help students investigate a text from various perspectives, encouraging them to share the tasks of making meaning and collaborating so they can assemble a complete understanding. The responsibility for understanding is a mutual event in this context.

The members of a group read a common text independently with a particular purpose in mind. The group then meets to discuss what they have read and they work together to build a collective understanding of the concept. Content area teachers frequently instruct in their subject area using the reciprocal teaching model to ensure each student has a solid understanding of the concept being taught. Several remediation programs have adopted the reciprocal model.

This practice is an orchestrated conversation between teachers and students, ultimately between students themselves, over segments of a nonfiction text. Conversation participants assume one of five roles: summarizer, question generator, clarifier, predictor, and leader. Each role requires that students adopt specific types of note-taking responsibilities to prepare them to take part in the discussion. Each student approaches the text from a slightly different angle and with a slightly different purpose.

Groupings

The teacher forms groups of five or six students who read at a similar level. Groups of six or seven members might include two students sharing responsibility for a role. The groups are generally formed according to the science or social studies concept being taught. Within a class, each group might investigate a different aspect of the common concept being studied. The groups conduct their studies, collect and compile their information, and then collaborate to pool information and generate a whole picture of the concept. Each member of the group assumes a different role each time the group meets. In this way, students become well rounded in their ability to investigate concepts from different points of view. Using diverse avenues of thinking becomes routine as students rotate through the roles.

Books

Science and social studies textbooks are generally used for reciprocal teaching lessons. However, nonfiction books on different reading levels that address the same concept may be used. Multiple texts might be used when the common textbook is too difficult for a particular class, as they often are. The content doesn't change; the books are all nonfiction, after all. The delivery, organization, level of detail, and ratio of visual supports to visual challenges (evident in such design elements as font size, amount of white space, number of illustrations, and use of headings, captions, and labels) of the original textbook may make a supplementary book appear easier to read. Recall that students might read at two different levels; the fiction level is generally one to three levels higher than the nonfiction level.

Training

Phase I

As with implementing literature circles, students learn their responsibilities during the training period known as phase I. Here, the teacher introduces students to the various roles, responsibilities, and routines of reciprocal teaching. It is wise to use a somewhat simple text, three or four levels lower than the group's nonfiction instructional level, during the training period. In this way, students are unencumbered as they become familiar with the workings of a reciprocal teaching lesson.

During phase I, the teacher trains all the members of the group in one role at a time. In other words, everyone learns how to be a summarizer at the same time. They all learn what to attend to while reading, how to annotate the text, what methods to use to record information, and how to share what they have found. Each role may require two or three days to sufficiently prepare the students to assume its responsibilities. Four roles that require a training period of two or three days each means the training period may last eight to twelve days; let's say that it will take two weeks to train a group to participate in reciprocal teaching. It is worth the time to fully instruct the group members at the beginning, rather than waste time later on trying to patch student understanding while groups limp along in their learning.

In the beginning, the teacher determines the length of the segment to be read and directly tells the students what kind of information they should attend to in their roles. Next, the students learn how to record salient bits of information using recording forms or note taking techniques. The teacher guides the students as they read and record the information. Finally, the teacher and the group discuss what they found in the text. In this last event, students also learn about conversation etiquette.

Since reciprocal teaching is used to help students investigate nonfiction texts, each member of the group might dedicate a notebook to recording information as they read within their role. The notebook also serves as the gathering point for information gleaned from the other members of the group. The epitome of collaborative note taking can be seen in a reciprocal teaching lesson in which students take notes based on what other students say during the discussion.

As students become more adept at reading and taking notes while reading, they begin to speak and question each other during the discussion. In this way, the specific roles begin to dissolve and students find themselves participating in a discussion over a concept they would probably never talk about without preparation. Similar to literature circles, the goal of reciprocal teaching instruction is to take students to a point where the roles no longer matter; students just read and discuss.

Roles

Each member of a reciprocal teaching group participates by adopting the particular responsibilities associated with an assigned role. It is important that students learn initially to operate only within their role and not to impinge on the other students' responsibilities. Each member of the group must be prepared to direct the other members of the group to specific places in the text. The discussion is always rooted in specific references to the text. Four text-based roles and a group leader are the group members for this mutual investigation of content text. They include:

- Summarizer
- Clarifier

- Question Generator
- Predictor
- Leader

Summarizer

The student in this role identifies and synthesizes the most important information in the text. This person determines the main ideas and key words. Headings, labels, titles, and captions are important sources of information for the summarizer. This person makes lists of key words and titles the lists using the main ideas recorded in his or her notebook. This person may make a list of the items labeled in an image and title the list with the name of the image; or copy the image and label it in the notebook. The summarizer often enumerates the items labeled such as, "A plant has four main parts: roots, stem, leaves, flower." The summarizer writes a summary that is generally a paragraph in length.

Summaries can be written at the sentence level, paragraph level, and section level. They are short, succinct, and general. In other words, a summary is less than a description, explanation, retelling, or recollection. Generally, a summary involves three parts—a section detailing who (Ben Franklin) or what (clouds) is being summarized; general information about where, when, and what happened; and prediction, question, comparison, contrast, transition to a continuation, or other conclusion. A summary may be three to nine sentences long, depending on what is being summarized and the text's length.

In reciprocal teaching lessons, the summarizer begins with a statement about the main idea, "This section explained the different types of clouds and what they mean for coming weather." The next part of a summary includes one to three sentences detailing what, when, where, and what happened, "Four types of clouds were described: cumulus, cirrus, nimbus, and cumulonimbus. Each type of cloud tells that a different kind of weather is coming." The last piece of a summary in a reciprocal teaching lesson might segue to the clarifier, "Britney will clarify each type of cloud and the type of weather it predicts. OK, Britney." The difficult part for the summarizer is to not reread or recount the section in too much detail. Students need to learn to not copy blocks of text from the book. This can be a hard habit to break once established.

The summarizer makes suggestions about what he or she thinks the other members of the group might write down in their notebooks—what he or she considers important. This might include the specific lists the summa-rizer has made, suggestions of sections of text to copy, and images labeled from the text.

Clarifier

The student in this role generally follows the summarizer and provides details about what the summarizer offered. For example, this student would describe what each kind of cloud looks like and explain what kind of weather each predicts. This member offers explanations and defini-tions (see chapter 4) of content words and ideas. Here is where students learn to use analogies and similes to simplify vocabulary and concepts. The clarifier is an important role because the clarifier forces the other students to make connections with other information.

It is important for the teacher to be on hand to ensure the veracity of the clarifications. Too many students believe in the "when in doubt make it up" philosophy. What students think is true, often is not. The other mem-bers of the group need to know that they can question the clarifier and ask for the student's source information ("because my cousin told me" is not adequate) or for verification from the teacher.

Notes from the clarifier sometimes involve the use of symbols as a short hand. For example, an equal sign in "cirrus clouds = gray bed sheets" means "cirrus clouds are gray and stretch across the sky like a gray bed sheet." Or, an arrow in "cirrus → rain" means "the presence of cirrus clouds mean it is going to rain soon."

Like the summarizer, the clarifier might suggest specific notes the oth-ers should record. Similarly, the clarifier needs to direct the other mem-bers of the group to look at specific places in the text. Page numbers should always accompany notes taken from text.

The clarifier is an important role, especially for false positive students. It enables students to recognize the various reasons why a text is difficult to understand, such as it introduces new or unfamiliar concepts, vocab-ulary words, and reference words. Students learn a number of strategies to help them achieve and maintain meaning. These include reread, restate, and ask for help.

Question Generator

The student in this role enables the other students to interact with spe-cific information and takes thinking to a higher plane. During the sum mary, the students first identify important information and form questions about it. The questions do not need to be answered or answerable. The object here is to get students to think beyond the text. The question generator helps students realize the text is just the beginning of learning. They learn that more information exists beyond the book; there is more to know than they know. As students learn to generate questions, they discover that answers may vary and some questions have no real answers; both realizations are life lessons. Questions do not necessarily have to be interrogatives. It is sometimes helpful to have students begin their question with, "I wonder."

Students operating within this role will find the "who, what, when, where, why, how, and what if" question stems useful. It may be helpful to introduce the list of questions described in chapter 5 when teaching students how to be the question generator. It is important to help students go beyond yes or no questions. Initially, students tend to ask low level questions and over time move to higher level questions. For example, "I wonder if there are other kinds of clouds not mentioned in the text." "I wonder how the clouds got their names." "I wonder who figured it out that certain kinds of clouds always meant that certain kind of weather is coming." "I wonder if the clouds happen in a certain order."

These types of questions are written in the student's notebook with a page number indicating where the information appeared that spawned the question. The question generator engages the other members of the group and encourages them to respond with what they think. This person also asks the other students if they have any questions. The questions are written down by the predictor, whose responsibilities are detailed below.

Predictor

The student in this role hypothesizes what will be discussed next in the book. The hypothesis may concern the micro level; that is, it may deal with context specifics, such as what will happen next. Or, the hypothesis may explore what the next concept may be. This student uses expository features such as headings, subheadings, and bold print to formulate predictions. For example, "I don't think we are going to find out who named the clouds in this book." Or, "I bet we could find out about clouds and tornadoes online."

Sometimes, the predictions take on a personal tone, "I don't think we need to know who named the clouds. Why would we ever need to know that, huh?" Or, "I bet Mr. Palmer is going to make us keep track of the different kinds of clouds we see each day this week."

Students in this role combine the information they have gleaned from the text with the knowledge they already hold in their schema. The other members of the group read, think, and discuss to confirm or discount the predictions.

Leader

Some groups have a designated leader. This person functions similarly to the discussion director in literature circles but does not ask questions. The leader keeps the group on task, moves them along, and ensures that every member is polite (reminding members to not interrupt, quelling unkind remarks, and so on). The leader is not exempt from reading the selection but is exempt from any kind of formal note-taking responsibilities. Being the leader is a big deal.

Phase II

The teacher is very much a part of the group during phase I. The teacher trains the students in each of the roles, teaches them how to prepare for discussion, and models and leads the discussions. Over time, the teacher becomes a less and less active group member. He or she slowly relinquishes the leadership to the students and contributes less and less. Phase II begins when the teacher finds him- or herself observing quietly and even occasionally walking away. At this point the students have internalized the rituals of reading, preparing, and discussing. The groups take on a life of their own during phase II. Eventually, the roles dissolve and the students read and discuss as adults do.

Essentially, reciprocal teaching takes students into and through the details of nonfiction text. It enables students to investigate concepts through a narrow lens and then allows them to collaborate to see the whole picture. This is a practice that also takes students beyond the text by giving them opportunities to connect what they have learned with what they already know or want to explore further. It's a powerful form of group engagement over nonfiction and informational texts.

As students acquire the tools of critical reading, reading instruction shifts over time to the writer's craft—the final area explored here.

9

Writer's Craft

Good instruction moves students beyond transitional guided reading so they can become truly fluent readers. Student comprehension improves as they learn to think about what they are reading. The texts they read increase not only in length, but in complexity and sophistication as well. As students continue to grow as readers, as they begin to read like writers, the focus of instruction continues to shift. The instruction attends more and more to elements of the writer's craft.

The writer's craft itself is a subject for study. The literary elements of character, setting, and plot take on a whole new meaning and purpose at this stage of development. At this stage, students study the art of writing. Truly fluent readers have the reading and thinking skills required to interact with the text on more than one level, for more than one purpose. Students at this stage of development become young literary scholars. They examine not just what happens in the text, but the steps and risks the author took to select and organize the words that became the tale. Literary elements, literary languages, literary structures, and literary devices are the author's raw materials. Truly fluent readers study these devices in instructional practices. The more students learn about writing while reading, the more likely the students are to use what they learned in their own writing.

Literary Elements

Character

Truly fluent readers learn to recognize not just who the major and minor characters are or who the antagonist and protagonist are. They learn to recognize character traits and indicators. Students learn that character traits are obvious references to appearance or behavior, as in, "He was seven feet tall." In other words, traits tell. Conversely, students learn that character indicators signify appearance, generally through behavior, as in the example, "He stooped to enter the room." The character's behavior indicates either he was very tall or the doorway was short. Students learn that character indicators require more engagement from the reader and therefore are more powerful. Character indicators show, not tell.

Truly fluent readers learn to track character development and character interplay. They observe how a character's behavior is influenced and how characters react to decisions made by other characters. Truly fluent readers observe how characters are shaped and reshaped as a story progresses. They learn to interpret motivation and recognize opportunities the characters take and miss. In other words, students begin to think of characters as real, multidimensional people, living out their lives between the pages of a book. Students at this level learn to distinguish major characters from minor characters and can explain why. They begin to distinguish between protagonists and antagonists.

Setting

Settings become more than just places. Readers begin to understand the importance of time as a dimension of setting. Teachers and students need to discuss time in the life of the characters, time measured by eons, the time of day and year, and time as a device to advance the plot and sculpt character. Students learn about the importance of weather and how it impacts characters, settings, and actions. Sensory images beyond the visual, such as smells, sounds, the feel of wind or air, and even the taste of salt in the air, all merge to give depth to setting. Students begin to realize how setting impacts the development of character and plot.

Plot

Types of Plot

As readers interact with many books, they encounter various types of plot structures. They might encounter parallel plots in which two story lines unfold concurrently. An example of this occurs in *Night Queen's Blue Velvet Dress*. One story line involves the main character and his grandmother. The second story line concerns the night queen and her king who are characters in a story the grandmother tells the boy over the course of a week. Just about every episode of a sitcom on television with an ensemble cast is written with a parallel plot. Other types of plots include cumulative plots in which new characters are introduced who repeat the same or similar actions throughout the tale. Examples of cumulative plots are "Little Red Hen," "The House that Jack Built," and "The Old Lady Who Swallowed a Fly." Circle plots are a third type. These stories end where they begin. Many traditional tales have such a structure. Attending to the details of plot points helps students structure their own stories.

Plot Points

All of this good writing must be situated somehow between the covers of a book. It must be organized into a coherent tale. Plot points are the major shifts in action in a narrative text. They form the framework of story; they give the text shape and purpose. Plot points move the story along. The other details of writer's craft, including character traits and indicators, dimensions of setting, and the language the author uses are all muscle and flesh on these ribs. Truly fluent readers learn to recognize plot points and understand how these points provide the structure or framework of a narrative.

Initiating Action

A story has to start somewhere. The initiating action is literally the beginning of the book. Generally, the first chapter is where the readers meet the main characters and find out where the story takes place and what it is like there. This is also when readers are introduced to the writer's style. The readers may hear voice in the writing or might perceive a specific tone or mood. So much rests on the opening sentence and paragraph. Often a reader's decision to continue with a book is made on the merit of the initiating action. A taut, quick-paced introduction foretells an enjoyable, snappy unfolding of story. However, a sluggish start may hint at a lethargic pace throughout the rest of the story.

Statement or Indication of Problem

Most times, a story isn't a story without a problem. In a book without a problem, the characters really have nothing to do, so why would anyone read this book? The problem is generally stated or indicated either near the end of the first chapter or in the second chapter. Sometimes when the problem occurs later on, it is unexpected, a shocker. A statement of problem is stated outright. A statement of problem is straightforward, something like, "The bank was robbed and the money was gone."

An indication of the problem, rather than a straightforward statement, requires more from the reader. The characters' behaviors or the weather or some other natural occurrence may suggest or hint that something has happened or is about to; the problem is inferred. In Ivy Ruckman's *Night of the Twisters*, for example, the subtle details in the description of the weather give hints of the coming problem. Like the literary differences between character indicators and character traits, stories with an indication of problem rather than a statement of problem are often considered to be better written. They require more skill on the part of the writer and engage more parts of the reader's schema. Like authors who use character indicators, authors who indicate the problem are more skilled writers. Readers who relish good writing, those who enter the story and lose themselves in it, appreciate the talent required to craft such text.

Rising Action

The third plot point is rising action. This is what makes a story a page-turner. Here, the characters try to solve the problem, but fail. They try. They fail. Tension builds. Twists and turns in the plot keep the reader engaged and thinking. New secondary characters may be introduced. The action zips along. The rising action may be one or several chapters long. Authors advance the story and keep the reader hooked during the rising action. Occasionally, readers get lost in rising action that becomes too complex or cumbersome. As students study various plot points, they learn to recognize good writing. If they can recognize it and talk about it, they can do it too.

Crisis

All that tension from the rising action has to lead somewhere, and it all leads here. The fourth plot point is the high point, the pinnacle of despair, the loss of all hope, the part of the story where the reader gasps, "Holy moly, they're all gonna die!"

If the story was a television show, it would end here with the words, "to be continued." The crisis provides the cliff-hanger. Generally, these chapters tend to be short, though not always. Punch, punch, and it's done. At this point in the story, students might analyze how the characters got to this point. What were the circumstances or combination of circumstances that allowed this to happen? Students might predict the characters' next actions. They can talk about the options the characters faces and understand that the author considered those options when writing the story. Throughout the story, truly fluent readers serve as pseudoeditors, critiquing and offering alternatives, all the while learning to recognize what good writing sounds like.

Resolution

Immediately after the crisis comes the resolution. When things are at their bleakest, the cavalry comes over the hill, the key is discovered under the mat, the storm abates, the bride says "no" at the altar. Problem solved—whew! The resolution either averts the crisis or solves it. The problem goes away either because of a character change or action development. The resolution may seem trite in series books, but it is frequently the hardest part of a narrative to write. The writer needs to save the day. Foreshadowing is sometimes used as a device to resolve the dilemma. Foreshadowing is where a seemingly inconsequential character or character's trait is mentioned early in the story. Then, when needed, the character or the character's trait saves the day. For example, a creepy, quiet gardener turns out to be a gemologist and identifies the jewel as a fake. Or, the hair ribbons that a character is always playing with come in handy when used to tie up the bad guy. The resolution doesn't have to be pleasant, however. Sometimes the resolution is a character's resignation to the fact of a situation.

Declining Action

The declining action follows the resolution. Everything must come to a close. Sometimes the declining action is woven into the resolution, rather than included as a separate development. Declining action ranges from good-natured chuckling of "aren't we clever" to the examination of the destruction after the storm. The declining action is the finishing of the tale. It is the aftermath of the crisis and resolution. It is the gathering of strands, the cleaning up of details, the explanation of what happened and how. The declining action takes place quickly and generally gets right to the point because the reader is nearly done reading the story. Depending on the tone of the story, the declining action may be a somber movement in the ending. Generally the story ends at this point.

Happily Ever After

"Happily ever after" is a euphemism for what happens after the end of the declining action, as not all stories have a fully articulated ending. A story may just dribble off after the resolution. Most often, the end of the declining action is the end of the story. However, some tales do carry on in epilogue to cinch off the literary elements, whether the characters ride off into the sunset, walk down the path, or sail away—whatever—the words "THE END" eventually appear.

These points combine to give shape and a logical sequence to a narrative text. They form the organization and sequence that makes up a story. The way the segments of a tale are arranged is so much more complex than what is generally studied in a story map work sheet. Newly fluent and truly fluent readers need to read a variety of texts with plot points following different sorts of events and structures. Students apprentice as writers as they analyze what professional writers do as they forge words into text. Students need to read a lot of short, excellent pieces to experience many writers and many types of texts. Through exploring the vast array of readings teachers provide, students learn what makes good writing good. These students learn from what they read, they begin to imitate style, and, by so doing, they hone their own craft.

Literary Languages

If words are colorful threads, what spools writers use! Idioms, "He couldn't make heads or tails of the directions"; similes, "The child was as good as gold during the service"; and colloquialisms, "You can't make a silk purse from a sow's ear," are the fibers that weave a rich literary textile (a metaphor; an extended or telescoping metaphor at that). Extended metaphors tend to go on and on, as in the example, "With each exhalation, noxious clouds of anger issued from Sister Noreen's maw as the toxic vapor of an egg salad and artichoke lunch choked us when she leaned in and prepared to breathe fire of hate and disdain."

Who knew so many kinds of metaphors existed? Some metaphors are implied, as in the example, "He shrank and disappeared into himself." And how easy is it to mix metaphors, "The advertisement lit a fire that drowned out the competition." Some metaphors have become so common they have a permanent place in our language. These dead metaphors include examples like, "stick of gum," "hero sandwich," "branch of government," and "girls' night out." What about metonyms? These take an attribute of an object and use it to refer to the object itself. Examples include, "the wide blue yonder" for the sky; or "out on the green," for the park. Synecdoche includes quips like, "the eagle flies on Friday," which means payday; or, "are you wearing heels?" which means high heel shoes. Synecdoche refers to a part of an object in substitution for the item itself.

An oxymoron is a delightful combination of opposites; for example, "deafening silence" or "military intelligence." Synesthesia refers to the mixing of words in two different senses as in "soft blue" or "sharp cheese." Personification is another language device writers use to embroider pictures, "The water giggled and chattered over the rocks in the shallow creek." Euphemisms are gentle words used to describe nasty items or tasks, as in, "the little boy's room" for "restroom."

Some literary languages are amusing. Spoonerisms occur when words collide, as in the example, "Our queer old Dean," when meaning, "Our dear old Queen." Onomatopoeia refers to a word whose pronunciation produces the sound that the word describes, as in the example, "Icy rain plink-plink-plinked against the glass." The reader knows exactly what that rain sounds like. Assonance refers to repeated vowel sounds used in a short passage, as in the example, "The cobbler hollered, 'This is awful. I can't call all the way down the hallway. Haul this, will you?'" Alliteration results when consonants are repeated among words in a series. For example, "His purple plumes postured proudly as he pranced through the park." Hyperbole is deliberate exaggeration; for example, "You could have knocked me over with a feather."

Chiasmus is an exotic use of words. Chiasmus often results in memorable bits of text. For example, "Ask not what your country can do for you. Ask what you can do for your country." Or, "Do unto others as you would have others do unto you." This type of statement powerfully shuffles words.

Language can be fun and funny, too. What about sarcasm, satire, parody, and irony? Writers use sarcasm to make a point by implying the opposite of what is said. For example, a father might respond to a teenage son's request to stay out all night by replying with, "Oh, sure, you can stay out all night. And be sure to drink too much, smoke, and don't forget to use drugs." A satire is a funny but mean kind of writing; the intention is to show a different perspective by skewing reality, but sometimes satire can be hurtful. A parody, on the other hand, is an imitation that gently pokes fun at the original writer or at the some other aspect of culture. Innovations on stories are examples of parodies. (For example, consider *The True Story of the Three Little Pigs* by Jon Scieszka.) Irony occurs when what is said is different from what is true. Irony only works, however, when the reader understands the difference. For example, "I play the drums at school and the violin elsewhere. Ha, who'd have thought that I play the violin?" The irony in this statement only works if the reader understands that the character can be easily imagined playing something loud and strong like drums but not something perceived as delicate like the violin.

Language gives life to text. Too often, however, the meaning and value of literary language choices are missed or misunderstood. Truly fluent readers are still children and still need to be guided as they read so they do not to overlook the gems words can be.

Once students are able to read, the job of teaching them reading skills doesn't end. Small group reading tools can enhance the comprehension skills of newly fluent and truly fluent readers.

Glossary

Ability group: the type of group used in traditional small group reading instruction. It is generally made of five to eight children who share a similar range of facility in reading texts. The makeup of these groups can change over the course of a year.

Aliteracy: a condition seen in newly fluent readers who can read, but choose not to.

Artifact: a written document, illustration, or other object produced by a student during, or following, the course of a lesson or task. A teacher can use these documents to evaluate a student's progress and calculate a student's grade.

Bottom power: the capacity of a reader to sit and participate in an event that he or she did not initiate, such as a guided reading lesson.

Challenges: features in a book that cause a reader to slow down and work harder.

Coaching statements: a type of teacher talk; positive statements made by the teacher that guide a reader's thinking by reminding the reader what he or she knows.

Comprehending skills: mental actions taken by a reader to connect the author's words with the meaning of the words in the reader's head, the meaning of the words in other texts, or the meaning of the words in the world at large.

Concept: what children learn about from reading the text; the theme in fiction, the content in nonfiction.

Content vocabulary: words directly related to the concept in a text.

Early: the third stage of literacy development; follows the preemergent and emergent stages. Early readers have learned to use strategies and are beginning to self-monitor.

Emergent: the second stage of literacy development; follows the preemergent stage. Emergent readers exhibit the six literacy behaviors needed to benefit from the first type of formal small group reading instruction, guided reading. This is the stage of development where strategies are learned.

Exemplar: a sample document or object provided by a teacher. Students can use these as models for their own projects or documents.

False positive readers: newly fluent readers who can read texts at the grade level but do not have a clue about what they read.

Familiar text: instructional text that covers concepts students can discuss before they read; it's written with 90 to 97 percent of words students can read, figure out, and understand and 90 to 97 percent of skills they can use.

Fluency: a multidimensional facet of reading made up of comprehending what is read, reading while self-monitoring for accuracy, reading smoothly with expression, and reading increasingly challenging text.

Guided reading: one of several types of small group practices used for reading instruction. It is the instructional practice used with emergent and early readers to teach reading strategies.

Homogeneous group: the type of group formation used for guided reading and transitional guided reading. Includes four to six children who know, use, and need to learn the same concepts, skills, and vocabulary words and who process text using the same strategies. Individuals may move out of a group and into another over the course of a year as they develop more quickly or fall behind other members of the group.

Instructional practice: any type of small group interaction between learners and an informed adult such as a teacher for the purpose of connecting new concepts, skills, vocabulary words, or strategy information to existing concepts, skills, vocabulary words, or strategy information. Features include the use of specifically selected texts or materials, direct, explicit instruction strategies, guided practice, and monitoring by the teacher.

Instructional text: any familiar text, generally a little book or longer picture book for use with any instructional practices, with a ratio of 90 to 95 percent supports to 5 to 10 percent challenges for fiction; 92 to 97 percent supports for nonfiction.

Literary elements: the characters, setting, and plot points that make up a fictional text.

Literature circles: one of several instructional practices for truly fluent readers that uses chapter books and novels. Roles and responsibilities distinguish this practice from others.

Little books: eight- to twelve-page books published by educational publishers for use in guided reading lessons with emergent and early readers.

Longer picture books: twelve- to thirty-eight-page books published by educational publishers for use in transitional guided reading lessons with newly fluent readers.

Metacognition: knowing what one knows; a reader needs to use metacognitive approaches to recognize the specific strategies used to make meaning.

Metacognitive teacher talk: coaching statements, questions, and prompts spoken by a teacher during and after the reading to make strategy use obvious to the readers so the strategies will be used again.

Newly fluent: the fourth stage of literacy development; follows the pre-emergent, emergent, and early stages. Newly fluent readers need transitional guided reading. Several types of newly fluent readers include aliterate or false positive readers, occasional, functional, interest, and social readers.

Phonemic awareness: the ability to distinguish between small units of sound within a linguistic stream.

Preemergent: the first stage of literacy development along the continuum, the stage in which readers learn how a language works. Preemergent readers develop the six literacy behaviors needed to benefit from guided reading during this stage of development: familiarity with the concepts of print, recognition of letter names, ability to distinguish between the sounds of letters and letter combinations, phonemic awareness, ability to recognize sight words, and fifteen minutes of bottom power.

Proficiency: the highest stage of literacy development. Readers at this stage of development are addicted to print and have an internal, self-fulfilling need to read.

Prompts: a type of teacher talk; statements that tell a reader what to do and provide a source of information.

Questions: a type of teacher talk; interrogatives used by a teacher to guide a reader's thinking, to encourage readers to self-monitor, or to help readers understand the source of information.

Reader's workshop: one of several instructional practices for truly fluent readers that uses chapter books and novels. The teacher orchestrates the reading with a minilesson and the children read the predetermined segment of text independently, complete a task or responsibility related to the minilesson, and return to the group prepared to discuss the reading and share their note-taking task.

Responses: oral, image, written, and three-dimensional actions taken by the reader to express understanding and revisit the concepts, skills, and vocabulary words found in the text.

Schema: the reader's previous experiences that act as a sieve to shape and inform his or her interpretations of new texts.

Self-monitoring: a reader's awareness that he or she does not understand the meaning of a text. It is the first layer of comprehending.

Shared reading: a read-together interaction between a whole or small group and a teacher using an enlarged text.

Sight words: high-utility, automatically recognized words, including environmental words.

Skills: isolated abilities that connect with other isolated abilities that contribute to a reader's fluency. Literacy skills include listening, speaking, reading, writing, observing, and representing. Reading and writing skills include phonics, grammar, and the conventions of print, such as punctuation, indentation, capitalization, and spelling. Study skills and comprehension skills are two additional types of skills.

Sources of information: ideas, words, grammar elements, phonics, and syntax elements a reader uses to problem solve while reading a text.

Strategies: the in-the-head problem-solving actions a reader takes to puzzle out words. Conscious decisions made by the reader to use one or more sources of information to make and maintain the meaning.

Study skills: actions taken by a reader to locate, record, retrieve, manipulate, and use information.

Talking points: places within the text or illustration that allow for various types of comprehending, such as inferring, predicting, comparing, and so on.

Teacher talk: specific coaching statements, questions, and prompts that guide readers' mental actions before and during the reading to encourage inquiry, and that guide readers' mental actions during and after the reading to encourage metacognition.

Teaching points: skills and vocabulary words within a text that are unfamiliar to the readers and form the instructional focus of the lesson.

TKWL chart: a version of the traditional KWL chart where the first column, "what do we know about" is reworked to "what do we think we know about."

Transitional guided reading: one of several small group instructional practices for reading instruction. The instructional practice for newly fluent readers, it focuses on comprehending the text as it is read.

Truly fluent: the fifth stage of literacy development; follows the preemergent, emergent, early, and newly fluent stages. Truly fluent readers can read, and they understand what they read. Instructional practices for these readers include reader's workshops, literature circles, reciprocal teaching, and various instructional practices that are designed to take children higher in their thinking and deeper in their understanding.

Resource Lists

Educational Organizations

Association for Supervision and Curriculum Development
1703 N. Beauregard Street
Alexandria, VA 22311
(800) 933-2723, ext. 2
www.ascd.org

International Reading Association
800 Barksdale Road
P.O. Box 8139
Newark, DE 19714
(800) 336-7323
www.reading.org

National Council of Teachers of English
1111 Kenyon Road
Urbana, IL 61801
(217) 328-3870
www.ncte.org

National Staff Development Council
5995 Fairfield Road, Suite 4
Oxford, OH 45056
(513) 523-6029
www.nsdc.org

Reading Recovery Council of North America
400 W. Wilson Bridge Rd., Suite 250
Worthington, Ohio 43085
(614) 310-7323
www.readingrecovery.org

Publishers of Transitional Guided Reading Materials

National Geographic School Publishing
1145 17th Street NW
Washington, DC 20036
(800) 368-2728
www.ngschoolpub.org

Newbridge Educational Publishing
P.O. Box 6002
Delran, NJ 08370
(800) 867-0307
www.newbridgeonline.com

Red Brick Learning
151 Good Counsel Drive
P.O. Box 669
Mankato, MN 56002
(800) 747-4992
www.redbricklearning.com

Rigby Education
Steck-Vaughn Company
Harcourt Achieve
6277 Sea Harbor Drive
Orlando, FL 32887
(800) 531-5015
www.harcourtachieve.com

Bibliography

Allen, Janet, and Kyle Gonzalez. *There's Room for Me Here: Literacy Workshop in the Middle School*. York, Maine: Stenhouse Publishers, 1998.

Allen, Janet. *Yellow Brick Roads: Shared and Guided Paths to Independent Reading 4–12*. Portland, Maine: Stenhouse Publishers, 2000.

Atwell, Nancie. *In the Middle: New Understandings About Writing, Reading, and Learning*. 2nd ed. Portsmouth, New Hampshire: Heinemann, 1998.

Beers, Kylene, and Barbara G. Samuels, eds. *Into Focus: Understanding and Creating Middle School Readers*. Norwood, Massachusetts: Christopher-Gordon, 1998.

Daniels, Harvey. *Literature Circles: Voice and Choice in the Student-Centered Classroom*. York, Maine: Stenhouse Publishers, 1994.

Daniels, Harvey and Nancy Steineke. *Mini-Lessons for Literature Circles*. Portsmouth, New Hampshire: Heinemann, 2004.

Dorn, Linda J., Cathy French, and Tammy Jones. *Apprenticeship in Literacy: Transitions Across Reading and Writing*. York, Maine: Stenhouse Publishers, 1998.

Fountas, Irene, and Gay Su Pinnell. *Guiding Readers and Writers 3–6: Teaching Comprehension, Genre and Content Literacy*. Portsmouth, New Hampshire: Heinemann, 2000.

Gambrell, L. B., and J. F. Almasi. *Lively Discussions*. Portsmouth, New Hampshire: Heinemann, 1996.

Gunning, Thomas G. *Best Books for Beginning Readers*. Boston: Allyn and Bacon, 1998.

Harvey, S., and A. Goudvis. *Strategies That Work: Teaching Comprehension to Enhance Understanding.* York, Maine: Stenhouse Publishers, 2000.

Harvey, Stephanie. *Nonfiction Matters: Reading, Writing and Research in Grades 3–8.* York, Maine: Stenhouse Publishers, 1998.

Hill, Bonnie Campbell, Nancy J. Johnson, and Katherine L. Schlick Noe. *Literature Circles and Response.* Norwood, Massachusetts: Christopher-Gordon, 1995.

Hoyt, Linda. *Make It Real: Strategies for Success with Informational Texts.* Portsmouth, New Hampshire: Heinemann, 2002.

————. *Revise, Reflect, Retell: Strategies for Improving Reading Comprehension.* Portsmouth, New Hampshire: Heinemann, 1999.

————, Margaret Mooney, and Brenda Parkes, eds. *Exploring Informational Texts: From Theory to Practice.* Portsmouth, New Hampshire: Heinemann, 2003.

Keene, Ellin, and S. Zimmermann. *Mosaic of Thought: Teaching Comprehension in a Reader's Workshop.* Portsmouth, New Hampshire: Heinemann, 1997.

Marzano, R. J., D. J. Pickering, and J. E. Pollock. *Classroom Instruction that Works: Research Based Strategies for Increasing Student Achievement.* Alexandria, Virginia: ASCD, 2001.

Marzano, R. J., J. S. Norford, D. E. Payter, D. J. Pickering, and B. B. Gaddy. *A Handbook for Classroom Instruction that Works.* Alexandria, Virginia: ASCD, 2001.

Moline, Steve. *I See What You Mean: Children at Work with Visual Information.* Portland, Maine: Stenhouse Publishers, 1995.

Ohanian, Susan. *Caught in the Middle: Nonstandard Kids and a Killing Curriculum.* Portsmouth, New Hampshire: Heinemann, 2001.

Optiz, Michael F., and Michael P. Ford. *Reaching Readers: Flexible and Innovative Strategies for Guided Reading.* Portsmouth, New Hampshire: Heinemann, 2001.

Palincsar, Annemarie, and Ann Brown. "Reciprocal Teaching: Activities to Promote 'Reading With Your Mind'" in *Reading, Thinking, and Concept Development*, edited by T. L. Harris and E. J. Cooper. New York: College Board Publications, 1985.

Pinnell, Gay Su, and Irene C. Fountas. *Leveled Books for Readers 3–6*. Portsmouth, New Hampshire: Heinemann, 2001.

Raphael, Taffy E., Marcella Kehus, and Karen Damphousse. *Book Club for Middle School*. Lawrence, Massachusetts: Small Planet Communications, Inc., 2001.

Raphael, Taffy E., Laura S. Pardo, and Kathy Highfield. *Book Club: A Literature-Based Curriculm*. 2nd ed. Lawrence, Massachusetts: Small Planet Communications, Inc., 2002.

Rasinski, Timothy, and Nancy Padak. *Effective Reading Strategies: Teaching Children Who Find Reading Difficult*. 2nd ed. Upper Saddle River, New Jersey: Merrill, 2000.

Rose, Laura. *Easy Reading*. Chicago: Zephyr Press, 2001.

Serafini, Frank and Cyndi Giorgis. *Reading Aloud and Beyond: Fostering the Intellectual Life with Older Readers*. Portsmouth, New Hampshire: Heinemann, 2003.

Tatum, Alfred W. *Teaching Reading to Black Adolescent Males: Closing the Acheivement Gap*. Portland, Maine: Stenhouse Publishers, 2005.

Wormeli, Rick. *Meet Me in the Middle*. Portland, Maine: Stenhouse Publishers, 2001.

Index

About the Author

Gail Saunders-Smith is a former class-room teacher and Reading Recovery teacher leader. She continued to work with children and teachers when she served as reading/language arts K–12 supervisor and coordinator of state and federal programs for the Summit County Board of Education in suburban Akron, Ohio. Gail is currently a national staff developer and writer. Much in demand as a lively and well-informed presenter, she has given workshops across the United States and Canada on all aspects of literacy development. Gail also has visited schools in Great Britain, New Zealand, Australia, and Russia.

Five of Gail's children's books have been published by Rigby, as well as a number of teacher support materials. Red Brick Learning has published forty-six of her nonfiction little books and five big books for emergent readers. She continues to serve as consulting editor for the company. Her first professional development book, *The Ultimate Guided Reading How-To Book,* is available from Zephyr Press. Gail also has published articles on early literacy development in a number of journals.

Gail holds a BS and MA in early childhood education, an MS in administration, and a PhD in curriculum and instruction. She describes herself as a reader, writer, student, and teacher.